Legal Education at the Crossroads

For several years, legal professions across the world have, to varying degrees, been undergoing dramatic changes as a result of a range of forces such as globalisation, diversification and changes in regulation. In many jurisdictions, the extent of these transformations have led to a process of professional fragmentation and generated uncertainty at institutional, organisational and individual levels about the nature and future of legal professionalism. As a result, legal education is in flux in many jurisdictions including the United States, the United Kingdom and Australia, with further effects in other common law and some civil law countries. The situation in the United Kingdom exemplifies the sense of uncertainty and crisis, with a growing number of pathways into law; an increasing surplus of law graduates to graduate entry positions; and, most recently, proposals for reform of legal education and training by the Solicitors Regulation Authority (SRA). This collection addresses both current and historical approaches showing that some problems which appear to be modern are endemic, that there are still some important prospects for change and that policy issues may be more important than the interests of lawyers and educators. This makes this book, which was previously published as a special issue of the *International Journal of the Legal Profession*, a source of interest to lawyers, law students, academic and policy makers as well as the discerning public.

Avrom Sherr is an Emeritus Professor and Director at the Institute of Advanced Legal Studies, University of London. His research focuses on legal education, the legal profession, access to justice, ethics and conduct of professions and professional competence.

Richard Moorhead is a Professor of Law and Professional Ethics and Vice Dean (Research) at the UCL Faculty of Laws. His research focuses on the legal profession, legal services, legal ethics, professional competence and access to justice.

Hilary Sommerlad is a Professor of Law and Social Justice at the School of Law, University of Leeds. Her research focuses on the legal profession, gender and diversity generally, and access to justice.

Legal Education at the Crossroads

Education and the Legal Profession

Edited by

Avrom Sherr, Richard Moorhead and Hilary Sommerlad

Routledge
Taylor & Francis Group
LONDON AND NEW YORK

First published 2017 by Routledge

2 Park Square, Milton Park, Abingdon, Oxfordshire OX14 4RN
52 Vanderbilt Avenue, New York, NY 10017

Routledge is an imprint of the Taylor & Francis Group, an informa business

First issued in paperback 2018

British Library Cataloguing in Publication Data
A catalogue record for this book is available from the British Library

ISBN 13: 978-1-138-22037-9 (hbk)
ISBN 13: 978-0-367-13918-6 (pbk)

Typeset in Plantin
by diacriTech, Chennai

Publisher's Note
The publisher accepts responsibility for any inconsistencies that may have arisen during the conversion of this book from journal articles to book chapters, namely the possible inclusion of journal terminology.

Disclaimer
Every effort has been made to contact copyright holders for their permission to reprint material in this book. The publishers would be grateful to hear from any copyright holder who is not here acknowledged and will undertake to rectify any errors or omissions in future editions of this book.

Contents

Citation Information

The chapters in this book were originally published in the *International Journal of the Legal Profession*, volume 22, issue 1 (March 2015). When citing this material, please use the original page numbering for each article, as follows:

Chapter 1

"You never want a serious crisis to go to waste." Reflections on the reform of legal education in the US, UK, and Australia
Richard L. Abel
International Journal of the Legal Profession, volume 22, issue 1 (March 2015) pp. 3–26

Chapter 2

From practical idealism to the ideology of the market: Whitehall, Westminster and higher education 1963–1983
Maureen Spencer
International Journal of the Legal Profession, volume 22, issue 1 (March 2015) pp. 27–49

Chapter 3

Legal education, ethics and access to justice: forging warriors for justice in a neo-liberal world
Donald Nicolson
International Journal of the Legal Profession, volume 22, issue 1 (March 2015) pp. 51–69

Chapter 4

The role of ADR in developing lawyers' practice: lessons from Australian legal education
Kathy Douglas
International Journal of the Legal Profession, volume 22, issue 1 (March 2015) pp. 71–86

Chapter 5

The LLB as a liberal degree? A re-assessment from an historical perspective
Patricia Leighton
International Journal of the Legal Profession, volume 22, issue 1 (March 2015) pp. 87–102

Chapter 6
Legal education without the law – lay clients as teachers and assessors in communication skills
Wilson Chow & Michael Ng
International Journal of the Legal Profession, volume 22, issue 1 (March 2015) pp. 103–126

Chapter 7
The National Lawyers College of the People's Republic of China
Roderick O'Brien
International Journal of the Legal Profession, volume 22, issue 1 (March 2015) pp. 127–132

Notes on Contributors

Richard L. Abel is Michael J. Connell Distinguished Professor of Law Emeritus at the UCLA School of Law, Los Angeles, USA.

Wilson Chow is an Associate Professor at the Faculty of Law, The University of Hong Kong, Hong Kong, China.

Kathy Douglas is the Deputy Head of Leaning & Teaching GSBL at the Graduate School of Business and Law, RMIT University, Melbourne, Australia.

Patricia Leighton is a Professor Emeritus at the University of South Wales, Pontypridd and IPAG Business School, Pontypridd, France.

Richard Moorhead is a Professor of Law and Professional Ethics, Vice Dean (Research), UCL Faculty of Laws, UK.

Donald Nicolson is a Professor in the School of Law, University of Strathclyde, Glasgow, UK.

Michael Ng is a Faculty Member at the Faculty of Law, The University of Hong Kong, Hong Kong, China.

Roderick O'Brien is based at the School of Management, University of South Australia, Adelaide, Australia.

Avrom Sherr is Emeritus Professor and Director at the Institute of Advanced Legal Studies, University of London, London, UK.

Hilary Sommerlad is a Professor of Law and Social Justice, School of Law, University of Leeds, Leeds, UK.

Maureen Spencer is an Associate Professor in Law at the School of Law, Middlesex University, London, UK.

"You never want a serious crisis to go to waste."[†] Reflections on the reform of legal education in the US, UK, and Australia

RICHARD L. ABEL
Michael J. Connell Distinguished Professor of Law Emeritus, UCLA School of Law, Los Angeles, USA

ABSTRACT *Scholarly and academic commentators have been warning of a "crisis" in American legal education since the beginning of the 2008 recession. This article critically examines what they mean by a "crisis", whether the evidence supports their claims, and the responses they propose.*

Cassandras dominate the discourse on American legal education (Shah, 2010; Thies, 2010; Matasar, 2011; Winston & Crandall, 2011; Bourne, 2012; Campos, 2012; Caplan, 2012; Barton, 2015; but see Mitchell, 2012).[1] A wide variety of people and institutions confidently pronounce doom: "American legal education is in crisis" (*New York Times*, 2011); "The American model of legal education is broken as a value proposition" (Graves, 2013); this is "a time of existential crisis for legal education" (Rutgers Newark law dean, Farmer, 2013); "There are going to be massive layoffs in law schools ... " (Professor William Henderson, quoted in Bronner, 2013a); legal academia's business model is "busted" (*Washington Post*, 2013); "There is almost universal agreement that the current system is broken" (ABA Task Force member Thomas Lyons, quoted in Bronner, 2013b); "The house is on fire" (ABA Task Force member Michael Downey, quoted in Bronner, 2013b); we are "deeper into the chaos that is our present lot in legal education" (AALS President and Northwestern University Law School Dean Daniel Rodriguez, 2014); legal

[†]Rahm Emanuel, Obama's Chief of Staff, speaking about the collapse of Lehman Brothers in November 2008.

education is "at the crossroads", perhaps even "in the crosshairs" (Rodriguez, 2014); "Law schools are in a death spiral. . . . In three years, a top law school will close" (Brown, 2015); "[M]ore than half" of today's law graduates "will not make a career practicing law" (Merritt, 2013, 2015). As late as October 2015 the *New York Times* repeated that law schools were in a "death spiral" in an editorial entitled "The Law School Debt Crisis" (*New York Times*, 2015). Scholars write books about "failing law schools" (Tamanaha, 2012a), "the lawyer bubble" (Harper, 2013a; see also Harper, 2013b), "the vanishing American lawyer" (Morgan, 2010), even "the end of lawyers"—to quote Britain's own Richard Susskind (2008).

But as Mark Twain said about reports of his death, these dire warnings may be premature. History offers numerous examples of eschatological error (Garth, 2013). In 1927, resisting the entry of immigrants' sons, Stanford Law School's dean declared: "we have more lawyers today than there is any legitimate need for" (although there were just a tenth as many as there are now) (Marion Rice Kirkwood, quoted in Reed, 2011). The Great Depression intensified this rhetoric (Walker, 2014). A California State Bar committee announced in 1933: "As to whether the bar in California is overcrowded, every lawyer knows the answer" (Abel, 1989, p. 55). Columbia Law School Dean Harlan Fiske Stone decried the "influx to the bar of greater numbers of the unfit" (by which he also meant immigrants' sons) (Auerbach, 1976, p. 107). Notables like Stone (1934), Adolf Berle (1933), and Karl Llewellyn (1933, 1938) railed against the growth of "law factories" (whose handful of lawyers would not even qualify as boutiques today) (Lundberg, 1939). In the 1970s and 1980s American commentators attributed the fact that their economy was lagging behind Japan's to the alleged superfluity of lawyers and a mythic litigation explosion. (Several decades later Japan returned the compliment by blaming its economic stagnation on too few lawyers.)[2] In the 1990s Yale Law School Dean Anthony Kronman (1993), Harvard Law Professor Mary Ann Glendon (1994), and lawyer statesman Sol M. Linowitz (1994) wrote books about the "lost lawyer", the "crisis in the legal profession", and "the betrayed profession". The ABA (1996) responded to the alleged "civility" crisis by creating a committee on professionalism.

Hearing such a chorus of crisis-talk, social constructivists suggest that we ask who is speaking and why they are doing so now. Those questions were pioneered by Stanley Cohen's analysis (1972) of Mods and Rockers and Joseph Gusfield's history (1963) of the American temperance movement. Other social scientists have examined moral panics over comic books, television, marijuana, fluoridation, and crack babies. When our third child was born in 1971, my wife and I were attacked by Zero Population Growth fundamentalists. I take some satisfaction in reading claims that the latest crisis is under-population (Wattenberg, 1987, 2004; Longman, 2005; Pearce, 2010; Last, 2014).[3] We used to fear exhausting fossil fuel; now climate change cautions us to leave resources unexploited. Contemporary politicians shamelessly exploit anxieties about immigration, the spread of Islam, and the threat to families from same-sex couples.

What exactly is the current crisis? Consider the following facts (Segal, 2013). Four new professional schools have just opened, on top of another 10 recently accredited. Total enrolment rose 35% in the last decade. Students pay as much as

US$63,000 a year. Demand for professional services is declining. Starting salaries recently fell 13% in real terms, to a median of just over US$45,000. Fewer than half of recent graduates found permanent employment, and those who did were burdened by an average educational debt three times their starting salary. Does all that sound familiar? But it describes veterinarians, not lawyers. Would you still call that a crisis?

Countries define the 'crisis' very differently. Let me start with the ABA Task Force (2014), composed of six practitioners and three each of judges, academics, and consumers. It noted that law school applications fell precipitously, from a high of 100,000 in 2004 to just over half that in 2013. Average law school enrolment fell by 99 students between 2010/11 and 2013/14; aggregate enrolment in autumn 2014 was down 28% from its 2010 peak, and applications were down 37% (Sloan, 2014n). Nearly three-quarters of accredited schools experienced enrolment declines—of more than a third at 18 lower tier schools. From 2013 to 2014 the number of applicants with low LSAT scores fell another 9%, while those with high LSATs were stable. The ABA blamed this on "dramatic ... probably structural" changes in the job market predating the 2008 recession. The Association for Legal Career Professionals reported that though 92% of 2007 law graduates had full-time paid positions after nine months, only 85% did in 2012 (Chemerinsky & Menkel-Meadow, 2014). Firms with 100–250 lawyers hired more than a third fewer lawyers in 2013 than in 2006; but firms with more than 250 lawyers hired only 1% fewer (Leipold, 2015) The effect was felt most severely in lower status schools (few of whose graduates get such jobs). The ABA saw this as a crisis first of law graduates and then of law schools. Qualifying as a lawyer cost too much, left students mired in debt, and failed to prepare them for practice. As an afterthought, the ABA noted that "poor and lower income populations remain underserved", and that lack of access "affects segments of the middle-income population as well".

If the crisis is disequilibrium between supply and demand, as the ABA argues, it may be transitory—a predictable if painful market correction, concentrated in the lowest ranked schools.[4] Nearly 40 years ago a Harvard economist explained why supply in professional labour markets—especially those for lawyers—responds slowly to fluctuations in demand (Freeman, 1975).[5] Indeed, just a year after the report of the ABA Task Force quoted above, a second ABA Task Force (2015, pp. 2–3) acknowledged the "important market corrections, many of which are still underway". The largest US firms increased recruitment in 2011 and have continued doing so every year (Stetz, 2014b). In 2013 they hired many more law students as summer associates and made almost as many permanent offers as they had before the recession (Sloan, 2014a, 2014b, 2014o; *National Jurist*, 2014a). As a result of contracting law school enrolment, several commentators have predicted that demand will soon exceed supply as graduating classes continue to shrink (*National Jurist*, 2013a; Graefe-Reich, 2014; Stetz, 2014b; but see Henderson, 2014). Ninety-three percent of 2015 graduates who had been summer associates in 2014 received entry-level offers, up from 69% in 2009 (NALP, 2015). Indeed, 60% of 2014 graduates had full-time jobs requiring bar passage 10 months after graduation, up from 57% a year earlier, because there were 6% fewer graduates seeking jobs (Sloan, 2015b). Inflation-adjusted take-home pay (net of taxes) of graduates employed by US law firms increased 59% between 1998 and 2011—74% for those who took advantage of the most flexible debt repayment plans (*National Jurist*, 2011). In 2014 large New York firms gave associates bonuses from US$15,000 to over US$100,000, an average of US$40,000 more than the previous year (Goldstein, 2014). In autumn 2014, more than half of firms made more summer associate offers than had a year earlier (Sloan, 2015a). Similar corrections occurred twice in the 1990s (in response to recession and the dot-com bubble) and again in 2005, three years before Lehman Brothers collapsed and the burst housing bubble rippled through the economy via mortgage securitisation. Some US law schools remain bullish: 46% of admissions officers expected applications for autumn 2015 to increase (Bronstad, 2014b). The decline in those taking the LSAT and applying to and enrolling in law school has been decreasing and may be bottoming out (Hansen, 2015; Solomon, 2015). There was barely any decline between 2013 and 2014, and LSAT administrations were increasing (Sloan, 2015c). Two law schools have merged, and two have been acquired, but six new law schools have opened since the recession (Ewing, 2011; ABA Task Force, 2015, p. 11).[6] Fordham recently moved into a new tower to let it increase enrolment by more than a third; Boston University lavished US$180 million on expansion and renovation; Quinnipiac spent US$50 million to enrol 500 students, even though it has fewer than 300; Arizona State moved into a US$129 million building with nearly twice as much space; North Texas Dallas College of Law received more than 600 applications to enrol 153 in its 2014 inaugural class (Qualters & Sloan, 2014; Sloan, 2014u). But Thomas Jefferson had to sell and lease back its building (unable to make loan payments); and enrolment—on which it relies for 95% of its income—fell from 348 in 2010 to 255 in 2013, while nearly half of those who entered in 2010 failed or transferred (*National Jurist*, 2014i, 2014n).

Other countries perceive legal education 'crises' that overlap with but differ from the American. The Foreword to the *Legal Education and Training Review* (LETR) spoke of "growing student numbers, the escalating costs of qualifications and difficulties in finding employment" (Webb *et al.*, 2013). But it attributed this in part to cuts in legal aid (which makes an insignificant contribution to the American market); and it called for "increasing efforts to promote diversity and social mobility within the workforce of providers of legal services". Demand for British legal services contracted less sharply: turnover in 2012/13 was virtually unchanged from 2010/11 (see also Fletcher, 2014). Australian critics saw the central problem as onerous government regulation preventing the large number of diverse law schools from responding promptly to market signals (Dow & Braithwaite, 2013). Critics in both countries blamed inadequate government support for pedagogic deficiencies and student preoccupation with material success.

I want to deconstruct the alleged crisis by unpacking four elements: resentment of lawyers; the cost of legal education; student debt; and ranking. Shakespeare repeatedly played on the animus against lawyers.[7] Lorenzo da Ponte made the fake notary in *Cosi fan Tutti* and Dr Bartolo, the lawyer in *Marriage of Figaro*, objects of ridicule. In the nineteenth century, Honoré Daumier savagely caricatured lawyers (Abel, 2007). The *Virginia Law Review* published an article asking rhetorically: "Are There Too Many Lawyers?" (Wickham, 1889). Thirty years after that an Italian politician wrote an article bluntly declaring there were "too many lawyers" (Pietro Calamandrei, quoted in Carmignani & Giacomelli, 2009). Partly to cushion the effect of the Depression, Nazi Germany expelled its many Jewish and its few female lawyers. Greece contemporaneously shut the door to new entrants. Marc Galanter (2005) has richly delineated how lawyer jokes express the public's complicated but overwhelmingly negative feelings toward lawyers.

Several factors contributed to rapid growth in the production of lawyers. Women, who had been virtually excluded from the profession through the 1960s, now join it in numbers equal to men. The democratisation of higher education lowered class barriers. In the US, affirmative action sought to redress centuries of racism. In the UK, legal aid allowed fledgling lawyers to establish practices. Large firms responded to increased client demand by hiring the top graduates of lower ranked law schools, which became more attractive to applicants.[8] The number of law students exploded in many countries. Australia aims to have 40% of 25–34-year-olds equipped with a first degree and abolished the cap on enrolment in law (Norton, 2013; Steel, 2013). Places in British law departments increased nearly fivefold in the 1960s and 1970s (Abel, 1988: Tables 3.8, 3.11) and then nearly doubled between 2000 and 2010 (Fletcher, 2013). In the 1980s just four Law Society colleges and several polytechnics taught the Solicitor's Final Exam course; three decades later 42 institutions offer it (Hamilton, 2014). In Israel the number of entering law students increased from 6,000 in 1996 to 15,000 just 10 years later (Ziv, 2012). Admissions to practice increased 2,000% between 1964 and 2010 (Zer-Gutman, 2012). The number of American law students tripled between 1963 and 2011 (Kritzer, 2012). From 1970 to 2009 law students increased nearly fourfold in Italy and more than fivefold in Spain. But there are striking exceptions. Canada did not open a single new law school between 1969 and 2013 (Levin & Alkoby, 2012). The number of French law students barely grew between 1970 and 2010. And in Britain, the number of newly qualified lawyers was limited by the bottleneck of apprenticeships required for law graduates: about one for every three aspiring barristers and one for every four hoping to become solicitors.[9]

These statistics document widespread, sometimes dramatic, growth. But is that a crisis? Are there too many lawyers now, or were there too few earlier? The ratio of population per lawyer varies greatly across countries, with Japan at one extreme (4,000) (Chan, 2012, p. 322) and Israel at the other (160) (Ziv, 2012, p. 177). There is convincing evidence that large numbers of Americans lack access to lawyers (Laird, 2014; Sandefur, 2014). Is there a right number? Would more lawyers increase competition and reduce prices? Increase access to justice? Make the profession more diverse? Lower quality? Boost or slow economic growth? We don't know.

The second definition of the 'crisis'—the rising cost of legal education—contradicts the first—too many lawyers—since high tuition discourages entry. How expensive is law school? The US is an outlier, costing upwards of US$80,000 a year, after an almost equally expensive four-year first degree. Tuition doubled in real dollars in both public and private institutions between 1985 and 2009 (Tamanaha, 2012a). But these cost figures are exaggerated by being based on list prices rather than net expenditure after financial aid. Between 1992 and 2014, net cost rose only 22% at private and 60%

at public undergraduate colleges (Leonhardt, 2014a). The net cost of law school did not change between 2009/10 and 2012/13 and may have fallen since then as schools have increased financial aid to maintain enrolment (*National Jurist*, 2014h). Other countries, which treat higher education as a public (if not universal) good, are much cheaper. British law students pay £9,000 a year, plus the vocational stage (or Graduate Diploma in Law), and living expenses. Most Australian students pay no more than a total of A$30,000, and many live at home (Council of Australian Law Deans, 2007).

A number of explanations have been advanced for the high cost of American legal education. Some say American law professors earn too much (Weiss, 2010). But though they are paid about 50% more than their British counterparts, American salaries have been declining as a proportion of total cost. Educational quality may have improved as the ratio of students to faculty was cut by about half between 1980 and 2012 (Leichter, 2014). Some blame inflation on faculty preoccupation with research at the expense of teaching. But the rate of inflation has been the same at elite universities and at community colleges (where faculty do no research) (Archibald & Feldman, 2011). And though American law teachers are paid more than colleagues in other disciplines, tuition has risen no faster in law schools than in undergraduate colleges (Ehrenberg, 2013). Economists have argued that it is difficult to achieve efficiency gains in the production of some services (e.g. Baumol & Baumol, 1984); and indeed, the costs of health care and day care have risen at a similar rate as education (Leonhardt, 2014a). Critics have blamed the ABA for over-regulation, but there is little evidence that this affects price (US Government Accountability Office, 2009).

Other explanations seem more plausible. The increasing cost of public law schools is directly related to the decline in state funding (Ehrenberg, 2013; Chokshi, 2014), which now represents just 7% of my own university's budget. Michigan, Berkeley, and Virginia law schools receive virtually no public funding; Minnesota is considering relinquishing it (Ewing, 2014). Nationwide, public undergraduate colleges received an average of US$8,600/student in 1988 but just US$6,100 in 2013—about a third as much controlling for inflation (Dynarski, 2014). Competition for rank clearly raises costs (ABA Section on Legal Education and Admissions to the Bar, 2010). And student loans have enabled this spending spree, just as shopping on the never-never fuelled post-war consumerism. We know that third-party payment allowed some fat-cat barristers to charge huge fees to the legal aid system and unscrupulous solicitors to mass-process personal injury and government benefit claims. In the US, Medicare has permitted some doctors to perform routine procedures on patients at four times the national average, specialists to increase their inflation-adjusted incomes by 50% in seven years, and just 2% of doctors to account for about a quarter of all Medicare payments (Abelson, 2013; Abelson & Cohen, 2014).

So it makes sense to turn to a third formulation of the crisis: educational debt. There are several ways of financing legal education: the state, private philanthropy (mainly alumni/ae contributions), students (employment before, during, and after law school), their families, and other students (through differential fees). There are arguments for and against each. State funding lowers class barriers but disproportionately benefits the privileged few who attend law school and rarely keeps pace with inflation, forcing cuts in services. Because the Australian federal government spends far less on law students than on those studying other subjects, law schools must rely on adjuncts, mostly practitioners, for much of the teaching (Council of Australian Law Deans, 2007). Private philanthropy can shape—and distort—both teaching and research, as E.P. Thompson (1970) warned more than 40 years ago. Single disease foundations leave 'orphan' diseases unstudied (Mnookin, 2014). Foreign governments have become major donors to Washington, DC think tanks, which seek to shape federal government policy (Lipton *et al.*, 2014). Italy has accepted US$34 million from Tod's (a luxury goods purveyor) to restore the Colosseum, US$4 million from the fashion brand Fendi to restore the Trevi Fountain, and US$2 million from the luxury brand Bulgari to renovate the Spanish Steps (Pianigiani & Yardley, 2014). Billionaires put their names on institutes at elite universities (Broad, 2014). Law schools are named after wealthy donors: Drexel became the Thomas R. Kline School of Law after he gave US$50 million (with the consent of Earle Mack, after whom it previously had been named following a gift of US$15 million); the University of Arizona renamed its law school after James E. Rogers after he gave it US$130 million; Chapman University named its law school after Dale E. Fowler following a US$55 million donation; the University of Maryland became Francis King Carey School of Law following a US$30 million gift; Indiana University Law School—Indianapolis changed its name to Robert H. McKinney after he gave US$24 million; and Hofstra University named its law school after Maurice A. Deane following a US$20 million gift (Martin, 2014b). Law schools steer graduates to lucrative careers in the hope of future donations. The scramble for *US News* rankings motivates law schools to give scholarships to students with high LSATs and GPAs rather than the neediest. Australian students tend to live at home (a family contribution) and work part-time (self-funding); but the highly competitive national job market makes both options less attractive in the US. Family funding reproduces class differences.

That leaves educational loans—an option that did not exist when I went to law school but now totals more than US$1 trillion, having overtaken credit card debt four years ago (Korki, 2014) [it now seems to have levelled off (Pérez-Peña, 2014a)]. The average indebtedness of law students increased about 25% in real dollars between 2001 and 2011 (Tamanaha, 2013). Is that a problem? Because fewer than four in a thousand Americans obtain a legal qualification, I believe that those who enjoy its considerable benefits should pay full freight. A recent study estimated that a law degree adds a million dollars to lifetime earnings (Simkovic & McIntyre, 2014). But can all law graduates repay their debts? The burden is heaviest among those from low-ranking schools, who have less chance of getting any job and earn lower salaries when they do (Tamanaha, 2012b, 2013; Lat, 2015).[10] Although the evidence is ambiguous, it is plausible that debt encourages graduates to maximise income rather than represent the underserved (Rothstein & Rouse, 2011). Although indebtedness is much lower in the UK and Australia, the much higher proportion of law graduates who do not become lawyers have fewer ways of repaying loans. Should repayment be capped or forgiven? For all below an income ceiling, or just those representing underserved populations?

Ranking aggravates many of the problems just described. Australia's league tables have relatively little effect on students, most of whom study and practise in their home states. Canadian law schools largely ignore *Macleans's* rankings. The Research Excellence Framework and its predecessor, the Research Assessment Exercise, have had profoundly perverse consequences in the UK. But none of these exerts nearly as malign an influence as *US News*. By shaping the behaviour of law students, teachers, schools, and even legal employers, *US News* has created an almost unbreakable feedback loop (Sauder & Espeland, 2006, 2009; Espeland & Sauder, 2007, 2009, forthcoming). Faculty members strive to move laterally in order to improve status and salary. Because the *US News* algorithm allocates 22.5% to 'selectivity', schools award 'merit' scholarships to buy students with high LSATs and UGPAs, shrink entering classes to eliminate the bottom of the distribution, admit more LL.M. students and first-year transfers (who pay full freight but do not count for rankings), and inflate the number of applications (Sloan, 2014c).[11] Since 20% of the formula is placement, measured by the proportion of those with jobs nine months after graduation, schools simply hire their own for that period.[12] Reputation, which accounts for 40%, was based on randomly selected respondents, only 9% of whom bothered to reply.[13] Schools seek to raise their visibility by inundating the more than 11,000 American law teachers with glossy mailings announcing every faculty appointment, even lectures that no recipient will attend. The arbitrariness of these measures turns the rankings into the children's game of 'Chutes and Ladders'.[14] Sudden declines produce massive drops in applications, flights by faculty, the firing of deans, and fickleness in alumni/ae donations—an often irreversible downward spiral. Upwardly mobile schools compete to lure faculty stars and lavish money on students, especially on programmes improving their job prospects—both strategies that raise costs (US Government Accountability Office, 2009; Daugherty *et al.*, 2010). Because, perversely, any increase in per capita expenditure elevates rankings, no matter how the money is spent, students buy rank with their tuition dollars (further reproducing class inequality). Alumni/ae retroactively valorise their degrees by donating to their almae matres, converting financial capital into cultural capital while reaping a tax deduction. Unsurprisingly, some schools falsified numbers in order to deceive both *US News* and prospective students (Trachtenberg, 2013). A few schools at the bottom simply refused to play the game. The Brooklyn Law School dean said "the *US News* rankings may be good for lining the cage of a parakeet, but as a road map for students, they're not useful" (Stewart, 2014). Another response has been the proliferation of rankings by other criteria, such as practical training offered (*National Jurist*, 2014e; Stetz, 2014a), Best Value according to *National Jurist* (2014f), and percentage of graduates hired or made partner by large firms (*National Law Journal*, 2014).[15] The ranking of law reviews (Albertson, 2014a), often by citation counts, intensifies the scramble by faculty to publish in the most prestigious journals, which in turn seek to enhance their ratings by soliciting articles from faculty at higher-ranked schools.

None of this is surprising; the massification of society, the difficulty of measuring the quality of an experiential commodity like education ex ante (or even ex post), and information overload all compel consumers to simplify decision-making.

Undergraduate colleges and majors are rated by the starting salaries of their graduates, with predictably dire consequences for liberal arts subjects. After President Obama urged the federal government to rank all colleges, his Deputy Under-Secretary of Education confidently asserted: "this is not so hard to get your mind around". Creating a measure of graduates' earnings was just "like rating a blender" (Shear, 2014). Six months later the Department of Education acknowledged it was more complicated and would require constant refinement (Pérez-Peña, 2014b). Consumers have grown accustomed to relying on peer judgments: Amazon reviews of books, Zagats and Chowhounds of restaurants, TripAdviser of travel, Yelp and Angie's List of services. Sixty websites evaluate the quality and price of medical care (*Economist*, 2014), but all these metrics can be gamed. The ABA Task Force (2014) rightly complained that "little of the information used in ranking formulas related to education outcomes or conventional measures of programmatic quality or value". Sadly, no one was listening. Law teachers are poorly situated to complain, hoist by our own petard. Just as we spend our lives evaluating students, only to be evaluated by them in return (through in-house instruments and the website Ratemyprofessor), so the institutions on which our status depends are ranked by others.

Responses to crises are as illuminating as their conceptualisations. In all three countries reformers have called for deregulation to let law schools innovate. This is more than a little ironic. The ABA Task Force (2014) urged its parent organisation to modify or eliminate standards and grant more variances in order to create "opportunities for experimentation". But the Task Force seemed ambivalent about trusting innovation to faculty, who jealously guard their decision-making authority, insist on long-term security, are obsessed with scholarship, and aggressively defend their status. In the UK, the Bar Standards Board, Solicitors Regulation Authority, and ILEX Professional Standards established LETR, which sought to "remove requirements in training regulations that unduly restrict the development of innovative and flexible pathways to qualification ..." (Webb *et al.*, 2013). In Australia, the Commonwealth government commissioned a report urging its own Tertiary Education Quality and Standards Agency to "support a high degree of autonomy" and regulate with a "light touch" (Dow & Braithwaite, 2013).

The heart of the matter, of course, is the content of changes made or proposed. Those in the US are a very mixed bag, full of contradictions, often reviving ideas and practices firmly rejected decades earlier. The first three deal with faculty.

(1) Replace full-time faculty with adjuncts, who are cheaper, teach only what they feel is needed in practice, and don't waste time on scholarship.[16] Most British universities relied on full-time practitioners before the 1960s, and many civil law faculties still do. Should that be revived or emulated? A related proposal to eliminate tenure (which adjuncts do not enjoy) was defeated by law teachers (Sloan, 2014d).

(2) Regulate or discourage faculty research. The ABA Task Force (2014) urged law schools to "develop and implement a plan to manage the extent of law school investment in faculty scholarly activity". The Illinois State Bar

Association (2013) went much further, proposing that hiring and promotion be based on letters from practitioners and judges, not peer review of scholarship. These first two proposals exemplify Abbott's theory (1988) that occupational categories—here practitioners and professors—compete for jurisdiction in terms of knowledge domains.

(3) Prune faculty, often with golden handshakes.[17] This cuts costs but also narrows the curriculum and enlarges class size. Reduce salaries. New England Law School's dean set an example by cutting his by 25%—from US$867,000 to just US$650,000 (Albertson, 2013). One study found that at the 25 public universities with the highest paid presidents, student debt and the use of adjunct teachers grew faster than the average for all public universities (Erwin & Wood, 2014). But schools with lower salaries can't buy stars to raise their *US News* rank.

The next seven proposals address students.

(4) Improve the information available to prospective students to let the market function more effectively (Weiss, 2012; ABA Task Force, 2014, p. 33, 2015, p. 40, 42).[18] But can this market be efficient? Or is it more like health care, whose consumers find it extremely difficult to choose among insurance plans or medical procedures? What information would help a 20-something plan a 40-year legal career?

(5) Shorten post-secondary education by cutting a year from the BA and another from the JD (Rodriguez & Estreicher, 2013; ABA Task Force, 2015, p. 12; see also *New York Times*, 2013a, 2014b; but see Chemerinsky & Menkel-Meadow, 2014). Not surprisingly, students love this (Sloan, 2014l). President Obama offered a casual endorsement, conceding it was "probably controversial, but what the heck" (*National Jurist*, 2013d). Justice Scalia promptly declared his "vigorous dissent" to a proposal that "rests on the premise that law school … ought to be—a trade school" (Baude, 2014). Justice Ginsburg concurred, fearing that two years would "reduce the respect, the notion that law is a learned profession" (Coyle, 2014). Nearly half a century ago William Twining made the argument that law schools should seek to produce a Pericles rather than a plumber.[19] Medical schools have been shortening training for a long time (Emanuel & Fuchs, 2012; Hartocollis, 2012). Law schools used to admit some students after three years of undergraduate study and are resuming the practice (Sloan, 2014e). About a dozen schools let students compress their studies into two years, although not all reduce tuition (*National Jurist*, 2013i, 2013j, 2014o; Karas, 2014; Sloan, 2014f). Ironically, the ABA waged a successful war for the seven-year qualification in the 1930s (Abel, 1989, ch. 3). Of course, there is no one best educational system (Tyack, 1974). After all, law is a three-year undergraduate degree in the UK, but South Korea, Japan, China, Australia, and South Africa are moving in the other direction, toward making law a postgraduate degree (e.g. Steel, 2013).

(6) Freeze or reduce tuition to increase enrolment (*National Jurist*, 2013e, 2013f, 2014b, 2014m; Albertson, 2014b, 2014d; Bronstad, 2014a; Martin, 2014a; Sloan, 2014g, 2014k; Stewart, 2014). The president of Roger Williams University boasted that its "reduced tuition rate makes RWU School of Law one of the best values on the east coast . . . ". La Verne University admitted that "we are, undoubtedly, seeking to increase enrolment" by cutting tuition. Other schools attract students through gimmicks, offering a Master of Legal Science degree after one year for those who dislike law school (Sloan, 2014j), or rebates to those who flunk out of law school or fail the bar exam (*National Jurist*, 2013h) or fail to find a full-time job nine months after graduation (Najarro, 2015). But is any of this fiscally sound? And are the larger classes this entails pedagogically desirable? Some critics urge schools to award only need-based scholarships, ending cross-subsidies of richer students by poorer (Stewart, 2014). But any school adopting these tactics will decline in rank.

(7) Formalise the role of the two tiers of law schools in reproducing the profession's hemispheres (Heinz & Laumann, 1982; Heinz *et al.*, 2005). Brian Tamanaha (now comfortably ensconced in the upper tier) made a big splash by advocating this (2012a; see also Jonakrait, 2006/07). The ABA Task Force (2014, pp. 23–24) seems to endorse it. But a century ago, when Alfred Reed made a similar proposal with the imprimatur of the Carnegie Foundation, the ABA quickly commissioned Elihu Root, an elite lawyer, to produce a report embracing the fiction of a unitary bar in order to stem the flood of "tens of thousands" of immigrants seeking to become lawyers (Abel, 1989, ch. 3). Champions of the two tiers contend that the legal problems of ordinary individuals are less complicated and important than those of corporations and the wealthy, a proposition that Gary Bellow demolished (1977). Such arguments only ensure that justice will remain unequal (Chambliss, 2013).

(8) Waive professional examinations for in-state law graduates (Albertson, 2014e; Sloan, 2014v). New Hampshire allows students to substitute apprenticeship; Iowa is considering joining Wisconsin in granting a diploma privilege to graduates of in-state schools (Olson, 2015a). In the 1930s, ironically, the ABA vigorously opposed this diploma privilege (Abel, 1989, p. 62), which tends to narrow the curriculum. Indeed, other countries are moving in the opposite direction. Independently, New York has joined 15 other states in adopting the Uniform Bar Examination, which allows those passing it to practise in all the adopting states. The state's chief judge observed that "employment prospects for recent graduates are still grim" and "there has to be portability with the law license around the country" (Clifford & McKinley, 2015). LETR urges a shift "from content-focused to outcomes-focused learning" (Webb *et al.*, 2013; Hardee, 2014). Australian law teachers rail against the constraints of the "Priestly 11" compulsory subjects (Steel, 2013). At the end of the day, there may not be that much difference, since many American critics want law schools to teach to the bar exam.[20]

(9) Devote more resources to finding employment for graduates (Sloan, 2014h). But this is a zero-sum competition with other schools and does nothing to enlarge the pool of jobs. It also tends to benefit the better students, who need it less. By contrast, more than a dozen schools have established "incubators" to prepare graduates for independent practice (Bronner, 2013c; *National Jurist*, 2013g, 2014j, 2014k, 2014l; Sloan, 2014r). This also signals a return to the days when graduates of lower tier schools hung out their shingles, selling insurance, real estate, or aluminium siding while waiting for business (Carlin, 1962). Incubators certainly are preferable to teaching law office management in law school, since few graduates today practise alone immediately after graduation and cannot do so in Britain.

(10) Cut enrolment (Albertson, 2014c).[21] Advocates claim that schools have been forced to admit unqualified students, pointing to declining bar passage rates (Olson, 2015b). (But the bar exam has never been validated as a measure of quality; and of course *no* state continues to assess quality during the half century for which most lawyers practise.) Some schools have done this to preserve their *US News* rank (while rationalising that the downsized institution was "probably closer to our mission" and they had rightly refused to admit "lower quality students in order to fill seats"). Long before the 'crisis', schools closed part-time evening programmes for the same reason. But of course this endangers a school's solvency by reducing its income, to say nothing of curtailing access: to the profession for aspirants and to justice for clients.[22]

Four more proposals address curriculum.

(11) Offer more courses on-line (Colbran & Gilding, 2014; Gerlach, 2014; *National Jurist*, 2014c). The ABA will allow one semester's worth (Sloan, 2014t). This could reduce cost and let students work in order to pay for their education. Embracing on-line courses, John Marshall Law School candidly declared: "we take a market-driven approach to course development and consider carefully what will set us apart from other programs". Any such move calls for empirical research on the differences between what students learn in classrooms and on-line. Again, the ABA waged a successful war against part-time law schools in the 1930s (Abel, 1989, pp. 51–62).

(12) The 'crisis' has stimulated a variety of curricular innovations (Daniels *et al.*, 2014): joint degrees (often compressed into fewer years) (*National Jurist*, 2014b, 2014d), semesters abroad and dual qualification in another country (nods to globalisation) (Chambliss, 2011/12; *National Jurist*, 2012, 2013l), and specialisation (reflecting differentiation within the profession). Seeking new sources of income, law schools are teaching undergraduates and other professionals (Bronner, 2013b; Sloan, 2014m) and expanding their own graduate programmes (whose students pay full tuition and receive no financial aid). The ABA Task Force on Financing Legal Education (2015, p. 42) urged the ABA to "encourage

experimentation by law schools" and give "serious and open-minded consideration" to requests for variances from ABA rules.

(13) Place more emphasis on teaching legal ethics (Webb *et al.*, 2013). Everyone wants more ethical lawyers, but there is no evidence that law school instruction produces them (Abel, 2008, 2010).

(14) The push for more experiential learning receives broader support than any other proposal (Webb *et al.*, 2013; ABA Task Force, 2014, p. 26; Schluger, 2014; Sloan, 2014p, 2014s; Council of Australian Law Deans, n.d.).[23] But the idea is hardly new. In 1879 an ABA Commission said it was "unjust to students, and a fraud on the public, to recommend them as practitioners until they reach some creditable degree at least of skill and knowledge" (cited in Spencer, 2012). In 1921 Alfred Z. Reed called "the failure of the modern American law school to make any adequate provision in its curriculum for practical training ... a remarkable educational anomaly" (Reed 1921). In 1933 Jerome Frank asked "Why Not a Clinical Lawyer-School?" (Frank 1933). His plea was echoed by the ABA's McCrate Report (1992) and the Carnegie Commission's recent report (Sullivan *et al.*, 2007). Students enthusiastically vote with their feet for clinical courses. But the necessarily small classes make law school more expensive; more clinical education is inconsistent with shortening the length of law school; and resorting to cheaper externships or requiring postgraduate apprenticeship (Farmer, 2013; *New York Times*, 2013b, 2014c; ABA Task Force, 2014, p. 27) reverts to a system that was rejected in the US a century ago and whose pedagogic value has repeatedly been questioned in the UK.[24] Lawyers continue to learn experientially throughout their 40–50 year careers. Given the ever-increasing variety of functions they perform, what is best learned in law school and what in practice?

The last two proposals purport to address access to justice.

(15) Mandatory pro bono work before admission to the bar (Barnard, 2012; State Bar of California, 2013; McKinley, 2014; New York Times, 2014a). Given inadequate and diminishing support for legal aid, pro bono services must play an increasingly important role in improving access to justice (Abel, 2009). But is this the best way to train new lawyers? Should novices learn at the expense of the poor? And why should only new lawyers have to perform pro bono work?

(16) The legal profession is becoming more interested in regulating paraprofessionals (Kritzer, 1998; Moorhead *et al.*, 2003; Francis, 2011). The ABA is accrediting paralegal education (ABA Task Force, 2014, p. 25). Washington State offers a limited licence to deliver legal services without lawyer supervision, partly because "you have these folks out there doing unauthorized practice, which is harming the public. The hope is to bring them under the tent" (Bronner, 2013b). The (British) National Association of Licensed Paralegals urges licensing in order "to reduce the number of small businesses operated by a variety of persons: struck-off

> solicitors, LPC or BPTC graduates, and those with no formal legal qualifications ... " (Hamilton, 2014). Regulation must walk a fine line between improving access to justice, ensuring quality, and creating yet another cartel (cf. Rhode, 1981; Merritt & Merritt, 2013). There are lessons to be learned from the challenges from the "sharing economy" to hotels by Airbnb and VRBO and taxis by Lyft and Uber, which may have driven down the price of medallions (Barro, 2014).

The American experience described above offers potential lessons for legal educators in other countries. Social institutions resemble supertankers, hard to start moving, turn, or stop. Inertia increases when the institutions are legal, since law draws much of its authority from the past. The 2008 recession jolted American law schools out of their complacency. Observers were quick to cry 'crisis'. But why did they focus on the plight of law schools and students rather than address other, arguably more pressing, crises, such as access to justice or the profession's chronic failure to reflect the demographics of the society it serves?

American legal education experienced a classic bubble in the decades preceding 2008. Large firms responded to increased demand by paying efficiency wages and broadening recruitment to lower-ranked schools whose top students were bright and hard-working; although many were the children of immigrants, the 1960s rights revolution had delegitimated status barriers. Few such students would win this prize; but its allure let lower-ranked schools expand and raise tuition, financed by borrowing. When the housing bubble burst, law schools and applicants were slow to respond. This could have been seen simply as an inevitable market adjustment: protracted (like the economic recovery itself) and inflicting real hardship on some (just as others lost jobs or homes) but remediable through loan forgiveness (just as the US could have helped home owners keep their underwater houses by forcing lenders to take a haircut). Instead, the 'crisis' provoked serious rethinking, perhaps because the professional project no longer could keep its promise of protecting members from market forces. One striking feature shared by many responses to the 'crisis' is the willingness to jettison controls over the production of lawyers, which the profession painfully erected nearly a century ago, just as the profession already had lost much of its control over production by lawyers following successful attacks on restrictive practices (Abel, 2003, ch. 5).

The shock impelled legal educators to ask fundamental questions. How many lawyers should we have? Nations have entrusted that decision to different entities: the market in the US, the profession through apprenticeship in the UK and Ontario, and the government in Australia (until recently). How much should legal education cost? What would we lose by cutting costs? Are those acceptable trade-offs? Who should pay? Should that depend on whether lawyers deploy their legal expertise for public or private ends? Stratified societies require mechanisms for allocating people to strata. Class, race, gender, religion, and national origin no longer are legitimate discriminants (although they remain powerful influences). In the name of efficiency, instead, we construct a hierarchy of educational institutions that purport to use meritocratic criteria to select and evaluate. Critics of the dominant ranking have no choice but to offer alternatives and hope they can compete in Holmes's marketplace of ideas.

The most difficult questions are those posed by Harry Arthurs (2014): education by and for whom, for what, when, and where? Is there a common core of knowledge and skills all lawyers must possess? How and when should we evaluate whether lawyers have acquired them? Given the constant intensification in the division of labour, when and how should lawyers learn the ever more specialised knowledge and skills they need? Should they be further certified? Licensed? Does the legal academy perform a distinct, and essential, role in offering a critical perspective and producing new knowledge (Freidson, 2001)? Finally, we need to anticipate change at a pace and in directions previously unimaginable. Political, economic, social, cultural, and environmental developments will profoundly affect the demand for law (Rubin, 2014). Paraprofessionals, businesses delivering legal services but managed by non-lawyers, and information technology will shape supply just as powerfully (Legal Services Board, 2013; Dagilyte & Coe, 2014; Hamilton, 2014; Leighton, 2014).[25] If the past is a foreign country, the future will be even more alien. And we are already there.

Disclosure statement

No potential conflict of interest was reported by the author.

Notes

[1] In March 2013, nearly 70 distinguished law professors across the political spectrum wrote the ABA Task Force to "draw attention to the problems confronting legal education". But the 'crisis' in legal education is dwarfed by that in graduate medical education, which received more than US$15 billion from the government in 2012 and comparable amounts ever since the introduction of Medicare in 1965 (Eden *et al.*, 2014).

[2] Japan has dramatically increased the production of *bengoshi* in recent years (Chan, 2012).

[3] At any given time some catastrophist is warning of too many or too few people (Mayhew, 2013).

[4] Total US employment in legal services (not just lawyers) fell from a peak of 1.123 million in 2004 to 1.075 million in 2010 before recovering to 1.134 million in 2013 (US Bureau of Labor Statistics, 2013).

[5] The Association of American Medical Colleges anticipates a shortfall of 45,000 primary care doctors and 46,000 specialists by 2020 (*New York Times*, 2014b).

[6] Indiana Institute of Technology (Fort Wayne), Duncan School of Law (Knoxville, Tennessee), Concordia University (Boise, Idaho), Belmont University (Nashville, Tennessee), Judge Paul Pressler School of Law (Shreveport, Louisiana), and University of North Texas Dallas College of Law.

[7] For example, *Henry VI, Part 2* and *The Merchant of Venice*.

[8] According to the National Association for Law Placement, firms with 100 lawyers or more hired 16% of law graduates in 1982, steadily increasing their share to 41% in 2008 before dropping sharply. But firms with more than 500 lawyers accounted for 21% of 2013 graduates hired by law firms, up from 16% in 2011 (Stetz, 2014b).

[9] Partly because of limited places in medical schools and residencies, osteopathy has exploded in the US, growing from 14 schools enrolling 4,940 students in 1980 to 30 schools with more than 23,000 in 2014, accounting for about 22% of all new doctors (Bergerjuly, 2014).

[10] Similarly, medical assistants may pay as much as a year's salary for their training, after which many find no jobs (Carey, 2014).

[11] UCLA was pleased that the class entering in 2013 tied for the sixth highest median LSAT and fifth highest median GPA; it maintained these medians in 2014 while enrolling 21 more students. In 2014 it enrolled a record 45 transfer students and 158 LL.M. students.

[12] University of California Hastings fell from 19th place in 1992 to 54th in 2014, mainly because fewer than half of its graduates had full-time permanent jobs requiring a law degree nine months after graduation. It responded by cutting enrolment and instituting new programmes (Chen, 2014).

[13] *US News* increased its response rate to 32% by asking schools to provide the names of 10 people who know it—replacing one distortion with another (Sloan, 2014c).

[14] Washington & Lee fell 17 places when the proportion of graduates in employment declined 6%. Wisconsin rose 10 places and Arizona State University 13 when their proportions rose 6% and 8%, respectively. Catholic University experienced the greatest decline, 27 places, when its acceptance rate rose from 36% to 55% because the number of applicants declined (Sloan, 2014c).

[15] The *New York Times* is poised to enter the college ranking game (Anderson, 2014).

[16] At Vermont Law School, eight full-time faculty members voluntarily became part-time (*National Jurist*, 2013b).

[17] Thomas Jefferson Law School made 12 redundant; eight accepted buyouts at New England Law School (*National Jurist*, 2013c); Washington & Lee cut 12 positions; Thomas M. Cooley laid off half its faculty and staff (Douglas-Gabriel, 2015).

[18] Since 2013, law school websites have disclosed graduate employment rates, scholarship retention, and tuition, among other data (Sloan, 2014t).

[19] Silicon Valley has no qualms about producing coders in a few weeks through intensive boot camps (Lewin, 2014).

[20] Pressure on law schools to ensure that a high proportion of graduates pass the bar exam—including the threat of losing ABA accreditation—accentuates this tendency (Sloan, 2014i).

[21] Cooley Law School admitted *no* new students to its Ann Arbor campus for autumn 2014 (*National Jurist*, 2014g).

[22] Undergraduate colleges are under growing pressure to increase the class diversity of their students (Leonhardt, 2014b).

[23] California will require 15 hours in order to take its bar exam; the ABA has recommended a minimum of six (*National Jurist*, 2013k; State Bar of California, 2013; Sloan, 2014d).

[24] The ABA rejected paid externships in part because of the "perceived tension between the obligations of someone who is a paid employee and a student" (Sloan, 2014q).

[25] Providers other than barristers or solicitors accounted for nearly a third of UK legal services turnover in 2010 (Fletcher, 2014).

References

Abbott, A.D. (1988) *The System of Professions: An Essay on the Division of Expert Labor* (Chicago, University of Chicago Press).

Abel, R.L. (1988) *The Legal Profession in England and Wales* (Oxford, Basil Blackwell).

Abel, R.L. (1989) *American Lawyers* (New York, Oxford University Press).

Abel, R.L. (2003) *English Lawyers Between Market and State: The Politics of Professionalism* (Oxford, Oxford University Press).

Abel, R.L. (2007) Review of Marc Galanter, *Lowering the Bar, Journal of Legal Education*, 57, pp. 130.

Abel, R.L. (2008) *Lawyers in the Dock: Learning from Attorney Disciplinary Cases* (New York, Oxford University Press).

Abel, R.L. (2009) State, market, philanthropy and self-help as legal services delivery mechanisms, in: R. Granfield & L. Mather (Eds) *Private Lawyers in the Public Interest: The Evolving Role of Pro Bono in the Legal Profession* (New York, Oxford University Press), pp. 295–307.

Abel, R.L. (2010) *Lawyers on Trial: Understanding Ethical Misconduct* (New York, Oxford University Press).

Abelson, R. (2013) U.S. settles accusations that doctors overtreated, *New York Times*, 4 January.

Abelson, R. & Cohen, S. (2014) Sliver of medicare doctors get big share of payouts, *New York Times*, 9 April.

Albertson, A. (2013) New England Law downsizing enrollment, faculty size, *National Jurist*, 11 November.

Albertson, A. (2014a) Best law reviews: Stanford tops list, *National Jurist*, 7 March.

Albertson, A. (2014b) Penn State to cut tuition by almost half for Penn. residents, *National Jurist*, 8 January.

Albertson, A. (2014c) Three law schools cut faculty, class size, *National Jurist*, 7 April.

Albertson, A. (2014d) Villanova doubles full tuition scholarships, makes curricular changes, *National Jurist*, 27 January.

Albertson, A. (2014e) Iowa may dump bar exam for UIowa and Drake grads, *National Jurist*, 17 January.

American Bar Association Section on Legal Education and Admissions to the Bar. (1992) *Report of the Task Force on Law Schools and the Profession: Narrowing the Gap* (McCrate Report) (Chicago, ABA).

American Bar Association Section on Legal Education and Admissions to the Bar. (2010) *Report of the Special Committee on the U.S. News and World Report Rankings* (Chicago, ABA).

American Bar Association Section on Legal Education and Admissions to the Bar, Professionalism Committee. (1996) *Teaching and Learning Professionalism* (Chicago, ABA).

American Bar Association Task Force on Financing Legal Education. (2015) *Report* (Chicago, ABA).

American Bar Association Task Force on the Future of Legal Education. (2014) *Report and Recommendations* (Chicago, ABA).

Anderson, N. (2014) New York Times reportedly entering the college-rating field, *Washington Post*, 5 September.

Archibald, R.B. & Feldman, D.H. (2011) *Why Does College Cost So Much?* (New York, Oxford University Press).

Arthurs, H.W. (2014) The future of law schools: three visions and a prediction, *Alberta Law Review*, 51, pp. 705.

Auerbach, J.S. (1976) *Unequal Justice: Lawyers and Social Change in Modern America* (New York, Oxford University Press).

Barnard, A. (2012) Top judge makes free legal work mandatory for joining state bar, *New York Times*, 1 May.

Barro, J. (2014) Under pressure from Uber, taxi medallion prices are plummeting, *New York Times*, 27 November.

Barton, B.H. (2015) *Glass Half Full: The Decline and Rebirth of the Legal Profession* (New York, Oxford University Press).

Baude, W. (2014) Justice Scalia's commencement speech at William & Mary law school, *Washington Post*, 16 May.

Baumol, W. & Baumol, H. (Eds) (1984) *Inflation and the Performing Arts* (New York, NYU Press).

Bellow, G. (1977) Turning solutions into problems: the legal aid experience, *NLADA Briefcase*, 34, pp. 106.

Bergerjuly, J. (2014) Osteopathic schools turn out nearly a quarter of all med school grads, *New York Times*, 29 July.

Berle, A.A. (1933) Modern legal profession, *Encyclopedia of the Social Sciences*, 9, pp. 340.

Bourne, R.W. (2012) The coming crash in legal education: how we got here and where we go now, *Creighton Law Review*, 45, pp. 651.

Broad, W. (2014) Billionaires with big ideas are privatizing American science, *New York Times*, 15 March.

Bronner, E. (2013a) Law schools' applications fall as costs rise and jobs are cut, *New York Times*, 30 January.

Bronner, E. (2013b) A call for drastic changes in educating new lawyers, *New York Times*, 10 February.

Bronner, E. (2013c) To place graduates, law schools are opening firms, *New York Times*, 7 March.

Bronstad, A. (2014a) Wayne Law freezing tuition, boosting scholarships, *National Law Journal*, 22 October.

Bronstad, A. (2014b) Law school admissions officers guardedly optimistic, *National Law Journal*, 28 October.

Brown, D. (2015) Law schools are in a death spiral, *Washington Post*, 9 March.

Campos, P. (2012) The crisis of the American law school, *Michigan Journal of Law Reform*, 46, p. 177.

Caplan, L. (2012) An existential crisis for law schools, *New York Times*, 14 July.

Carey, K. (2014) When education doesn't deliver on its promise, *New York Times*, 5 October.

Carlin, J. (1962) *Lawyers on Their Own: A Study of Individual Practitioners in Chicago* (New Brunswick, NJ, Rutgers University Press).

Carmignani, A. & Giacomelli, S. (2009) *Too Many Lawyers: Litigation in Italian Civil Courts*. http://ssrn.com/abstracts=1431986.

Chambliss, E. (2011/12) Organizational alliances by U.S. law schools, *Fordham Law Review*, 80, p. 2615.

Chambliss, E. (2013) It's not about us: beyond the job market critique of U.S. law schools, *Georgetown Journal of Legal Ethics*, 26, p. 423.

Chan, K.-W. (2012) Setting the limits: who controls the size of the legal profession in Japan? *International Journal of the Legal Profession*, 19, pp. 321–337.

Chemerinsky, E. & Menkel-Meadow, C. (2014) Don't skimp on legal training, *New York Times*, 15 April.

Chen, V. (2014) The careerist: you can get into any (mid-rank) law school! *American Lawyer*, 16 July.

Chokshi, N. (2014) Map: where the average student loan burden is largest, *Washington Post*, 8 May.

Clifford, S. & McKinley, J.C. (2015) New York to adopt a uniform bar exam used in 15 other states, *New York Times*, 5 May.

Cohen, S. (1972) *Folk Devils and Moral Panics: The creation of the Mods and Rockers* (London, MacGibbon & Kee).

Colbran, S. & Gilding, A. (2014) MOOCs and the rise of online legal education, *Journal of Legal Education*, 63, p. 405.

Council of Australian Law Deans. (2007) *Review of the Impact of the Higher Education Support Act 2003: Funding Cluster Mechanism: Submission* (Sydney, CALD).

Council of Australian Law Deans. (n.d.) *Review of Australian Higher Education: Questions for Discussion: CALD Submission* (Sydney, CALD).

Coyle, M. (2014) Ginsburg on rulings, race, *National Law Journal*, 22 August.

Dagilyte, E. & Coe, P. (2014) Professionalism in higher education: important not only for lawyers, *Law Teacher*, 48, pp. 33–50.

Daniels, S., Katz, M. & Sullivan, W. (2014) Analyzing Carnegie's reach: the contingent nature of innovation, *Journal of Legal Education*, 63, p. 585.

Daugherty, M. et al. (2010) *American Bar Association Report of the Special Committee on the U.S. News and World Report Rankings* (Chicago, ABA).

Douglas-Gabriel, D. (2015) Why law schools area losing relevance—and how they're trying to win it back, *Washington Post*, 20 April.

Dow, K.L. & Braithwaite, V. (2013) *Report: Review of Higher Education Regulation* (Canberra, Commonwealth of Australia).

Dynarski, S. (2014) Why federal college ratings won't rein in tuition, *New York Times*, 20 September.

Economist. (2014) DocAdvisor, *The Economist*, 26 July.

Eden, J., Berwick, D. & Wilensky, G. (Eds) (2014) *Graduate Medical Education That Meets the Nation's Health Needs* (Washington, DC, National Academies Press).

Ehrenberg, R.G. (2013) American law schools in a time of transition, *Journal of Legal Education*, 63, p. 98.

Emanuel, E.J. & Fuchs, V.R. (2012) Shortening medical training by 30%, *Journal of the American Medical Association*, 307, p. 1143.

Erwin, A. & Wood, M. (2014) *The One Percent at State U: How University Presidents Profit from Rising Student Debt and Low-Wage Faculty Labor* (Washington, DC, Institute for Policy Studies).

Espeland, W. & Sauder, M. (2007) Rankings and reactivity: how public measures recreate social worlds, *American Journal of Sociology*, 113, pp. 1–40.

Espeland, W. & Sauder, M. (2009) How rankings affect diversity, *Southern California Review of Law and Social Justice*, 18, p. 587.

Espeland, W. & Sauder, M. (forthcoming) *Fear of Falling: How Media Rankings Changed Legal Education in America* (New York, Russell Sage Foundation).
Ewing, E. (2011) Indiana Tech to open law school, *National Jurist*, 25 May.
Ewing, E. (2014) University of Minnesota considers ditching public funding, *National Jurist*, 13 July.
Farmer, J.J. Jr. (2013) To practice law, apprentice first, *New York Times*, 17 February.
Fletcher, N. (2013) *Trends in the Solicitors' Profession: Annual Statistical Report* (London, Law Society).
Fletcher, N. (2014) Solicitors and the legal services market: change, the future and uncertainty (presented at W.G. Hart Workshop).
Francis, A. (2011) *At the Edge of Law: Emergent and Divergent Models of Legal Professionalism* (Farnham, Ashgate).
Frank, J. (1933) Why not a clinical lawyer-school? *University of Pennsylvania Law Review*, 81, p. 907.
Freeman, R. (1975) Legal "cobwebs": a recursive model of the market for new lawyers, *Review of Economics and Statistics*, 57, p. 171.
Freidson, E. (2001) *Professionalism, the Third Logic* (Chicago, University of Chicago Press).
Galanter, M. (2005) *Lowering the Bar: Lawyer Jokes and Legal Culture* (Madison, University of Wisconsin Press).
Garth, B. (2013) Crises, crisis rhetoric and competition in legal education: a sociological perspective on the (latest) crisis of the legal profession and legal education, *Stanford Law & Policy Review*, 29, p. 503.
Gerlach, M. (2014) William Mitchell Law School offers hybrid JD program, *National Law Journal*, 9 April.
Glendon, M.A. (1994) *A Nation under Lawyers: How the Crisis in the Legal Profession Is Transforming America* (New York, Farrar, Straus & Giroux).
Goldstein, M. (2014) Big law firms bring back hefty bonuses for associates, *New York Times*, 2 December.
Graefe-Reich, R. (2014) Keep calm and carry on, *Georgetown Journal of Legal Ethics*, 27, p. 55.
Graves, J. (2013) An essay on rebuilding and renewal in American legal education, *Touro Law Review*, 29, p. 375.
Gusfield, J. (1963) *Symbolic Crusade: Status Politics and the American Temperance Movement* (Urbana, University of Illinois Press).
Hamilton, A. (2014) In an ever-changing legal landscape, paralegals are the way forward, *Law Teacher*, 48, pp. 104–113.
Hansen, M. (2015) Count off, *American Bar Association Journal*, 64, March.
Hardee, M. (2014) To prescribe or not to prescribe? That is the question, *Law Teacher*, 48, pp. 69–78.
Harper, S.J. (2013a) *The Lawyer Bubble: A Profession in Crisis* (New York, Basic Books).
Harper, S.J. (2013b) Tyranny of the billable hour, *New York Times*, 29 March.
Hartocollis, A. (2012) N.Y.U. and other medical schools offer shorter course in training, for less tuition, *New York Times*, 23 December.
Heinz, J.P. & Laumann, E.O. (1982) *Chicago Lawyers: The Social Structure of the Bar* (New York, Russell Sage Foundation; Chicago, American Bar Foundation).
Heinz, J.P., Nelson, R.L., Sandefur, R.L. & Laumann, E.O. (2005) *Urban Lawyers: The New Social Structure of the Bar* (Chicago, University of Chicago Press).
Henderson, W. (2014) Letting go of old ideas, *Michigan Law Review*, 114, p. 201.
Illinois State Bar Association, Special Committee on the Impact of Law School Debt on the Delivery of Legal Services. (2013) *Final Report & Recommendations* (Chicago, Illinois State Bar Association).
Jonakrait, R.N. (2006/07) The two hemispheres of legal education and the rise and fall of local law schools, *New York Law School Law Review*, 51, p. 862.
Karas, T. (2014) Touro Law School becomes latest to offer two-year J.D., *New York Law Journal*, 7 March.
Korki, P. (2014) Ripple effects from rising student debt, *New York Times*, 25 May.
Kritzer, H.M. (1998) *Legal Advocacy: Lawyers and Nonlawyers at Work* (Ann Arbor, University of Michigan Press).
Kritzer, H.M. (2012) It's the law schools stupid! Explaining the continuing increase in the number of lawyers, *International Journal of the Legal Profession*, 19, pp. 209–225.
Kronman, A. (1993) *The Lost Lawyer: Failing Ideals of the Legal Profession* (Cambridge, MA, Belknap Press).

Laird, L. (2014, October) Too many lawyers? Not here. In rural America, lawyers are few and far between, *American Bar Association Journal*, 100, p. 36.

Last, J.V. (2014) *What to Expect When No One's Expecting: America's Coming Demographic Disaster* (Jackson, Tenn, Encounter).

Lat, D. (2015) Law school is way too expensive. And only the federal government can fix that, *Washington Post*, 8 April.

Legal Services Board. (2013) *Evaluation: Changes in Competition in Different Legal Markets: An Empirical Analysis* (London, LSB).

Leichter, M. (2014) Changes to law school standards eliminate waste, *American Lawyer*, 30 September.

Leighton, P. (2014) Back from the future: did the LETR really prepare us for the future? *Law Teacher*, 48, pp. 79–93.

Leipold, J. (2015) An introduction to the entry-level legal employment market (paper presented at UCLA Law School 21 January).

Leonhardt, D. (2014a) How the government exaggerates the cost of college, *New York Times*, 29 July.

Leonhardt, D. (2014b) Top colleges that enroll rich, middle class and poor, *New York Times*, 8 September.

Levin, A. & Alkoby, A. (2012) Is access to the profession access to justice? Lessons from Canada, *International Journal of the Legal Profession*, 19, pp. 283–299.

Lewin, T. (2014) Web-era trade schools, feeding a need for code, *New York Times*, 13 October.

Linowitz, S.M. (1994) *The Betrayed Profession: Lawyering at the End of the Twentieth Century* (New York, C. Scribner's & Sons).

Lipton, E., Williams, B. & Confessore, N. (2014) Foreign powers buy influence at think tanks, *New York Times*, 6 September.

Llewellyn, K.N. (1933) The bar specializes—with what result? *The Annals*, 166, p. 177.

Llewellyn, K.N. (1938) The bar's troubles, and poultices. And cures? *Law & Contemporary Problems*, 5, p. 104.

Longman, P. (2005) *The Empty Cradle: How Falling Birthrates Threaten World Prosperity, and What to Do about It* (New York, Basic Books).

Lundberg, F. (1939) The law factories: brains of the status quo, *Harper's*, 179, p. 180.

Martin, L. (2014a) University of La Verne cuts tuition by 35%, to no longer offer scholarships, *National Jurist*, 7 April.

Martin, L. (2014b) Drexel changes name, adds trial advocacy focus after $50M donation, *National Jurist*, 22 September.

Matasar, R.A. (2011) The viability of the law degree: cost, value, and intrinsic worth, *Iowa Law Review*, 96, p. 1579.

Mayhew, R.J. (2013) *Malthus: The Life and Legacies of an Untimely Prophet* (Cambridge, Harvard University Press).

McKinley, J.C. (2014) New York State's top judge permits early bar exam in exchange for pro bono work, *New York Times*, 11 February.

Merritt, D.J. (2013) The job gap, the money gap, and the responsibility of legal education, *Washington University Journal of Law & Policy*, 41, p. 1.

Merritt, D.J. (2015) What happened to the class of 2010? Empirical evidence of structural change in the legal profession. http://ssrn/com/abstract=2577272.

Merritt, D.J. & Merritt, D.C. (2013) Unleashinng market forces in legal education and the legal profession, *Georgetown Journal of Legal Ethics*, 26, p. 367.

Mitchell, L.E. (2012) Law school is worth the money, *New York Times*, 28 November.

Mnookin, S. (2014) One of a kind, *New Yorker* 32, 21 July.

Moorhead, R., Sherr, A. & Paterson, A. (2003) Contesting professionalism: legal aid and nonlawyers in England and Wales, *Law & Society Review*, 37, pp. 765–808.

Morgan, T. (2010) *The Vanishing American Lawyer* (New York, Oxford University Press).

Najarro, I. (2015) Brooklyn Law School offers a safety net for new students, *New York Times*, 13 July.

National Association for Law Placement. (2015) *Perspectives on fall 2014 law student recruiting* (Washington, DC, NALP).

National Jurist. (2011) Recent law grads enjoy better standard of living than 10 years ago, *National Jurist*, 22 June.

National Jurist. (2012) NYU revamps third year curriculum, *National Jurist*, 2 November.
National Jurist. (2013a) Why there will be more jobs than graduates by 2016, *National Jurist*, 29 November.
National Jurist. (2013b) Vermont, Seton Hall take first public moves to reduce faculty size, *National Jurist*, 15 July.
National Jurist. (2013c) Schools begin to report lower enrollment numbers, *National Jurist*, 26 August.
National Jurist. (2013d) Obama calls for two-year JD, schools already working on it, *National Jurist*, 9 September.
National Jurist. (2013e) UCincy, others cut non-resident tuition, *National Jurist*, 12 July.
National Jurist. (2013f) George Mason freezes tuition for three years, *National Jurist*, 12 December.
National Jurist. (2013g) ASU starts law firm to employ, train recent grads, *National Jurist*, 22 March.
National Jurist. (2013h) Florida Coastal assures success in law school and on bar exam, *National Jurist*, 15 March.
National Jurist. (2013i) At Charlotte School of Law, get in, get out faster, *National Jurist*, 1 March.
National Jurist. (2013j) NYLS offers accelerated JD honors program, *National Jurist*, 17 September.
National Jurist. (2013k) Whittier launches new experiential curriculum, *National Jurist*, 16 July.
National Jurist. (2013l) ASU to prepare JD students for Canadian bar, *National Jurist*, 10 March.
National Jurist. (2014a) Law firm fall recruitment better, but still largely flat, *National Jurist*, 24 February.
National Jurist. (2014b) Suffolk: earn JD and tax LLM in 3 years, *National Jurist*, 9 April.
National Jurist. (2014c) William Mitchell gets ABA approval to offer first hybrid online/on-campus JD, *National Jurist*, 8 January.
National Jurist. (2014d) Boston U. offers MD/JD in six years, *National Jurist*, 28 February.
National Jurist. (2014e) Best practical training schools for part-time students, *National Jurist*, 18 June.
National Jurist. (2014f) Best Value law schools: 6 new private schools make list, *National Jurist*, 13 June.
National Jurist. (2014g) No 1L students at Cooley's' Ann Arbor campus this fall, *National Jurist*, 2 July.
National Jurist. (2014h) Net cost of law school has been flat, could drop, *National Jurist*, 3 October.
National Jurist. (2014i) Why creditors are unlikely to foreclose on Thomas Jefferson, *National Jurist*, 24 September.
National Jurist. (2014j) UMass launches law incubator, *National Jurist*, 30 September.
National Jurist. (2014k) Monterey College of Law launches program for new solo attorneys, *National Jurist*, 30 September.
National Jurist. (2014l) Loyola Law New Orleans launches solo practitioner incubator, *National Jurist*, 3 October.
National Jurist. (2014m) Wayne State freezes tuition, offers scholarship to all students, *National Jurist*, 24 October.
National Jurist. (2014n) Thomas Jefferson sells building, claims solid financial footing, *National Jurist*, 29 October.
National Jurist. (2014o) Elon cuts law school to 2.5 years, adds residency program, *National Jurist*, 9 October.
National Law Journal. (2014) Ranking the go to law schools, *National Law Journal*, 24 February
New York Times. (2011) Legal education reform, *New York Times*, 25 November.
New York Times. (2013a) How much law school is enough? *New York Times*, 25 January.
New York Times. (2013b) Starting out: the lawyer's apprentice, *New York Times*, 24 February.
New York Times. (2014a) Better lawyering for the poor, *New York Times*, 27 February.
New York Times. (2014b) Bottlenecks in training doctors, *New York Times*, 19 July.
New York Times. (2014c) Room for debate, *New York Times*, 31 July.
New York Times. (2015) The law school debt crisis, *New York Times*, 24 October.
Norton, A. (2013) *Keep the Caps Off! Student Access and Choice in Higher Education* (Melbourne, Grattan Institute).
Olson, E. (2015a) Bar exam, the standard to become a lawyer, comes under fire, *New York Times*, 19 March.
Olson, E. (2015b) Study cites lower standards in law school admissions, *New York Times*, 27 October.
Pearce, F. (2010) *The Coming Population Crash* (Boston, Beacon Press).

Pérez-Peña, R. (2014a) Financial pressures ease on students, studies say, *New York Times*, 13 November.
Pérez-Peña, R. (2014b) Rating plan would put colleges into one of three categories, *New York Times*, 19 December.
Pianigiani, G. & Yardley, J. (2014) Corporate Medicis to the rescue, *New York Times*, 15 July.
Qualters, S. & Sloan, P. (2014) Law schools: growth, retrenchment, *National Law Journal*, 29 December.
Reed, A.Z. (1921) *Training for the Public Profession of the Law* (New York, Carnegie Foundation).
Reed, J.W. (2011) On being watched: modeling the profession during uncertain times, *Bar Examiner*, June, p. 6.
Rhode, D. (1981) Policing the professional monopoly: a constitutional and empirical analysis of unauthorized practice prohibitions, *Stanford Law Review*, 34, p. 1.
Rodriguez, D.B. (2014) AALS presidential address, *AALS News*, April, p. 1.
Rodriguez, D.B. & Estreicher, S. (2013) Make law schools earn a third year, *New York Times*, 18 January.
Rothstein, J. & Rouse, C. (2011) Constrained after college: student loans and early-career occupational choices, *Journal of Public Economics*, 95, pp. 149–163.
Rubin, E. (2014) The future and legal education: are law schools failing and, if so, how? *Law & Social Inquiry*, 39, pp. 499–521.
Sandefur, B. (2014) Accessing justice in the contemporary USA: findings from the Community Needs and Services Study, *Researching Law*, 24(4), p. 2 (Fall).
Sauder, M. & Espeland, W. (2006) Strength in numbers? The advantages of multiple rankings, *Indiana Law Journal*, 81, p. 205.
Sauder, M. & Espeland, W. (2009) The discipline of rankings: tight coupling and organizational change, *American Sociological Review*, 74, pp. 63–82.
Schluger, K. (2014) Conn. task force calls for legal education reforms, *Connecticut Law Tribune*, 17 June.
Segal, D. (2013) High debt and falling demand trap new vets, *New York Times*, 23 February.
Shah, M. (2010) The legal education bubble: how law schools should respond to changes in the legal market, *Georgetown Journal of Legal Ethics*, 23, p. 843.
Shear, M.D. (2014) Colleges rattled as Obama seeks rating system, *New York Times*, 26 May.
Simkovic, M. & McIntyre, F. (2014) The economic value of a law degree, *Journal of Legal Studies*, 43, pp. 249–289.
Sloan, K. (2014a) Associate Hiring: "two steps forward, one step back", *National Law Journal*, 19 February.
Sloan, K. (2014b) Theory: the time was never better to enroll in law school, *National Law Journal*, 16 April.
Sloan, K. (2014c) Once again, U.S. News ranks Yale no. 1 law school, *National Law Journal*, 10 March.
Sloan, K. (2014d) ABA Council abandons bid to drop tenure requirement, *National Law Journal*, 17 March.
Sloan, K. (2014e) Hastings, Iowa add accelerated law degree programs, *National Law Journal*, 25 March.
Sloan, K. (2014f) Arizona's early bar exam sitting attracts 38 hopefuls, *National Law Journal*, 14 April.
Sloan, K. (2014g) La Verne offers flat-rate law school tuition, *National Law Journal*, 26 March.
Sloan, K. (2014h) It's their job to find the jobs for law students, *National Law Journal*, 24 February.
Sloan, K. (2014i) Panel near decision on law schools' bar exam passage rates, *National Law Journal*, 6 February.
Sloan, K. (2014j) "Risk-free" J.D. offers students a one-year escape hatch, *National Law Journal*, 11 March.
Sloan, K. (2014k) Movement to lower law school tuition gains steam, *National Law Journal*, 27 February.
Sloan, K. (2014l) Support among prospective law students for fast-track law school, *National Law Journal*, 11 February.
Sloan, K. (2014m) University of Arizona first to offer BA in law, *National Law Journal*, 7 May.
Sloan, K. (2014n) Law school enrollment slump continues, *National Law Journal*, 21 July.
Sloan, K. (2014o) Market struggles to absorb record law school class of '13, *National Law Journal*, 19 June.
Sloan, K. (2014p) Legal educators plot the future of real-world learning, *National Law Journal*, 17 June.
Sloan, K. (2014q) ABA Council says no to paid law student externships, *National Law Journal*, 10 June.
Sloan, K. (2014r) Vermont incubator to place lawyers in underserved areas, *National Law Journal*, 1 July.
Sloan, K. (2014s) Boston University to offer real-world training to 1Ls, *National Law Journal*, 2 July.
Sloan, K. (2014t) Legal education due for a makeover, *National Law Journal*, 4 August.

Sloan, K. (2014u) Law schools continue to build out, *National Law Journal*, 22 September.
Sloan, K. (2014v) Iowa weighs dropping bar exam for in-state law graduates, *National Law Journal*, 27 August.
Sloan, K. (2015a) Summer-associate hiring increases for fifth straight year, *National Law Journal*, 4 March.
Sloan, K. (2015b) Law school grads' job rate rises—but there's a catch, *National Law Journal*, 29 April.
Sloan, K. (2015c) Has law school enrollment hit rock bottom?, *National Law Journal*, 20 July.
Solomon, S. (2015) Despite forecasts of doom, signs of life in the legal industry, *New York Times*, 1 April.
Spencer, A.B. (2012) The law school critique in historical perspective, *Washington & Lee Law Review*, 69, p. 1949.
State Bar of California, Task Force on Admissions Regulation Reform: Phase 1. (2013) *Final Report* (San Francisco, State Bar of California).
Steel, A. (2013) *LSSSE in Australia: The UNSW Results* (Sydney, UNSW).
Stetz, M. (2014a) Best schools for practical training, *National Jurist*, 33 March.
Stetz, M. (2014b) Is Big Law hiring again? *National Jurist*, 8 September/October.
Stewart, J.B. (2014) A bold bid to combat a crisis in legal education, *New York Times*, 5 April.
Stone, H.F. (1934) The public influence of the bar, *Harvard Law Review*, 48, p. 1.
Sullivan, W.M., Colby, A., Wegner, J.W., Bond, L. & Shulman, L.S. (2007) *Educating Lawyers: Preparation for the Profession of Law* (Carnegie Report) (New York, Carnegie Foundation).
Susskind, R. (2008) *The End of Lawyers? Rethinking the Nature of Legal Services* (New York, Oxford University Press).
Tamanaha, B.Z. (2012a) *Failing Law Schools* (Chicago, University of Chicago Press).
Tamanaha, B.Z. (2012b) The quickly exploding law graduate debt disaster, *National Jurist*, 18 April.
Tamanaha, B.Z. (2013) Problematic state of legal education (paper presented at the Law and Society Association annual meeting, Boston, June).
Thies, Daniel. (2010) Rethinking legal education in hard times: the recession, practical legal education, and the new job market, *Journal of Legal Education*, 59, p. 598.
Thompson, E.P. (1970) *Warwick University Ltd: Industry, Management and the Universities* (Harmondsworth, Penguin).
Trachtenberg, B. (2013) Law school marketing and legal ethics, *Nebraska Law Review*, 91, p. 866.
Tyack, D.B. (1974) *The One Best System: A History of American Urban Education* (Cambridge, MA, Harvard University Press).
U.S. Bureau of Labor Statistics. (2013) *NAICS 541100–Legal Services* (Washington, DC, BLS).
U.S. Government Accountability Office. (2009) *Higher Education Issues Related to Law School Cost and Access* (Washington, DC, GAO).
Walker, A. (2014) Bramble Bush Revisited: Llewellyn, the Great Depression, and the first law school crisis, 1929–1939, *Journal of Legal Education*, 64, p. 145.
Washington Post. (2013) Our shrinking law schools, *Washington Post*, 3 February.
Wattenberg, B. (1987) *The Birth Dearth* (New York, Pharos Books).
Wattenberg, B. (2004) *Fewer: How the New Demography of Depopulation Will Shape Our Future* (Chicago, Ivan R. Dee).
Webb, J., Ching, J., Maharg, P. & Sherr, A. (2013) *Setting Standards: The Future of Legal Services Education and Training Regulation in England and Wales* (London, Legal Education and Training Review).
Weiss, D.C. (2010) Study partly blames higher law school tuition on 40% leap in faculty size, *American Bar Association Journal Daily News*, 30 March.
Weiss, D.C. (2012) No fudging: revised standard bars law schools from publishing misleading consumer information, *American Bar Association Journal*, 6 August.
Wickham, J.J. (1889) Are there too many lawyers? *Virginia Law Review*, 13, p. 879.
Winston, C.C.M. & Crandall, R.W. (2011) *First Thing We Do, Let's Deregulate All the Lawyers* (Washington, DC, Brookings Institution).
Zer-Gutman, L. (2012) Effects of the acceleration in the number of lawyers in Israel, *International Journal of the Legal Profession*, 19, pp. 247–263.
Ziv, N. (2012) Unauthorized practice of law and the production of lawyers, *International Journal of the Legal Profession*, 19, pp. 175–192.

From practical idealism to the ideology of the market: Whitehall, Westminster and higher education 1963–1983

MAUREEN SPENCER
School of Law, Middlesex University, London, UK

ABSTRACT *Drawing predominantly on Cabinet and departmental papers in the National Archives, the article reviews ministers' and civil servants' changing perceptions of the objectives of higher education in the decades between the Macmillan and Thatcher administrations. It gives an overview of two major reports, the 1963 Robbins Report on Higher Education and the 1971 Ormrod Report on Legal Education and suggests that some unresolved dichotomies are contained within their predominantly humanistic philosophy. It concludes with an examination of the launch of the Thatcher administration's embrace of an overtly market-based ideology in the early 1980s. A key document is a report prepared in 1983 for Prime Minister Thatcher by the Cabinet Office's Think Tank, the Central Policy Review Staff (CPRS). The Report on Higher Education is in a series of files titled 'Responsiveness of Higher Education to Market Forces and Employment Needs'. The commissioning of the Report, newly released under the thirty year rule, suggests that Thatcher took a keener personal interest in higher education than historians had hitherto appreciated. Universities and colleges were early targets for the implementation of market-based reforms in public institutions. The article concludes by arguing that official reticence in addressing the theoretical underpinnings of concepts of the public good from the 1960s onwards contributed to making higher education all the more vulnerable to the inroads from the neo-liberal consumerist ideology articulated in the CPRS Report.*

Introduction

"If academic lawyers are to be taken seriously as educators", writes Twining, "surely understanding the higher education system, including its financing, should be part of our expertise". He adds "Our current arrangements have been fashioned by history" (2014, p. 96, p. 99). This article sheds new light on the evolution of post-compulsory education in the second half of the twentieth century. The 1963 Report of the Committee on Higher Education (CHE, 1963) (hereafter CHE), chaired by Lord Robbins, gave intellectual legitimacy to state subsidised expansion of higher education institutions. Some eight years later, Ormrod, Chair of the Committee on Legal Education, (CLE, 1971) (hereafter CLE) endorsing the liberal humanism of Robbins, advocated extending the role of these publicly funded bodies in the provision of academic legal education. Both reports in other words were influenced by the post-war welfarist concepts which prevailed until the 1970s.[1] However within ten years this ideology was under challenge from the neo-liberal programme of the Thatcher administration. By the early 1980s, what the historian of higher education policy, Michael Shattock, has called "... a long march from a fully subsidised higher education system to a substantially privatised one" was in its stride (2012, p. 7).[2] Research based on recently opened government papers in the National Archives reveals the contributions of senior civil servants and ministers in successive administrations from Macmillan to Thatcher to that trajectory.

The retreat from Robbins's values, however, has been a largely unacknowledged one. No subsequent administration has dared to distance itself explicitly from his report. The Coalition Government claimed to be preserving his legacy while asserting it was making it relevant in today's more stringent economic climate. In a pamphlet published to mark the fiftieth anniversary of the publication of the Report, Willetts, then Minister for Higher Education, applauded its philosophical stance. He wrote,

> Robbins achieved a perfect equipoise between utilitarian arguments and confident appeals to underlying value ... the Robbins report exudes a confidence in the broad value of higher education. He is in no doubt that study at this level is inherently worthwhile – a belief which remains true today whether the subject is history or particle physics. He sees higher education as part of a wider education for citizenship. This is also as true today as it was then. (2013, p. 17)

The principles set out in the Robbins Report have proved an enduring prism through which politicians and administrators still claim to review and present policy changes in higher education, although their practice became more and more prompted by the private than the public good value of higher education. It seems therefore that the Robbins Report has served differing policy objectives. The article, outlining a typology of the principles advocated in the Report, suggests that it could do so since these principles enshrined a number of unresolved contradictions. A review of the declassified departmental papers reveals how the executive, both politicians and civil servants, addressed these contradictions in implementing policy. It is argued that both Whitehall and Westminster made only a cursory examination of the social objectives of higher education in the wake of the publication of the Report. In other words, what Williams has called the "Robbins's aspirations" were asserted rather than explained in official discourse in the 1960s (2013, p. 70). In contrast to such limited theoretical analysis, a sustained and coherent exposition of individual consumerist values in higher education is to be found in a recently released internal government report presented to Prime Minister Thatcher in July 1983 by the Central Policy Review Staff

(CPRS). Their research was unambiguously titled 'Responsiveness of Higher Education to Market Forces and Employment Needs'.[3] The article suggests that earlier reticence on the part of ministers and officials in articulating public good values in the 1960s, a time when the economic climate was favourable to increased state intervention, contributed to making higher education all the more vulnerable to the market ideology which took hold in the 1980s. By then the worsening of the national and global economic situation provided the context for retrenchment in the public realm.

Robbins, 'idealistic but very practical'

The intention of the Robbins Committee, appointed by Treasury Minute in February 1961, was to set out the foundational principles of higher education. Its underlying philosophy was crystallised in Chapter Two of the Report, titled 'Aims and principles'. This posed the question, "... what purposes, what general social ends should be served by higher education?" (CHE, p. 5). Robbins's answer is contained in four famous paragraphs:

> Para 25. We begin with instruction in skills suitable to play a part in the general division of labour ....
> Para 26. But secondly, while emphasising that there is no betrayal of values when institutions of higher education teach what will be of some practical use, we must postulate that what is taught should be taught in such a way as to promote the general powers of the mind ....
> Para 27. Thirdly we must name the advancement of learning ....
> Para 28. Finally there is a function that is more difficult to describe concisely but that is none the less fundamental: the transmission of a common culture and common standards of citizenship. (CHE, pp. 6–7)

Alongside these objectives, the Report is infused with references to the foundational principles of higher education, including for example a whole chapter on academic freedom. Robbins, according to his biographer, was determined the Report should have an underlying philosophy which would be "... 'idealistic but very practical' and everything should be argued out in terms of evidence" (Howson, 2011, p. 862). Robbins himself had some differences with traditional concepts of liberal education. He was dismissive of Cardinal Newman's *The Idea of a University*. He wrote:

> I found much of it – its repudiation of utility, its hostility to research, its subordination of all disciplines to theology – positively repellent .... [I]t convinced me that to attempt to describe our objectives in terms of any single aim must necessarily be invalid and misleading. (p. 862)

But difficulties in achieving such an admirable pluralism were to emerge and some early reaction of academics to Robbins was quite negative. An editorial in the *Universities Quarterly*, commenting on 'The Perspectives of Robbins', described the Report as "... an oddly one-dimensional and transient document". It was critical of its potentially divisive implications and its emphasis on vocationalism, commenting that,

> The Report does not offer to discuss in any serious way the function of the university. Or rather, since it certainly proposes a job-directed function for higher education, how is vocation related to purpose, and how is this relation to be expressed in terms of intellectual-academic studies?[4]

This suggests that, for some at least, Robbins's broad ranging analysis contained some unresolved, and maybe irreconcilable, questions. The next section looks in more detail at how the Robbins Report addressed the implementation of the aims it identified and draws out three possible sets of dichotomies.

Dichotomies

Utility/knowledge for its own sake

The first of the Robbins aims for higher education is phrased in utilitarian language, namely training in skills. However this sits alongside the next two more intellectual objectives, to 'promote the general powers of the mind' and 'the advancement of learning'. Accompanying the disinterested pursuit of knowledge, the contrasting theme of utility as an objective is reflected in two aspects in the Report, namely specific training in vocational subjects and an acknowledgement of the contribution to the economy made by higher education. The Report famously rejected the 'man-power planning' approach to recruitment to higher education. It noted

> ... while it is possible for a number of professions and over a short term, to calculate with a fair degree of precision what the national needs for recruits will be, we have found no reliable basis for reckoning the totality of such needs over a long term. (CHE, p. 48)

The contribution of universities to the economy was to be in the more general context of 'investment' in 'human capital' since "To devote resources to the training of young people may be, *au fond*, as much entitled to be considered a process of investment as devoting resources to directly productive capital goods" (p. 204). The Report identified the need to introduce new courses, including setting up postgraduate business schools and investing in the expansion of scientific and technological education while also noting " ... any decline or weakening in the study of the humanities would impoverish the intellectual and spiritual life of the country" (p. 165). Acknowledging both the economic and emancipatory aspects of higher education for individuals and society, the Report asserted the importance of remembering " ... that the goal is not productivity as such but the good life that productivity makes possible" (p. 204). Apart from such bland generalities, the Report had little to say about the specific place of the growing number of graduates in society as a whole. The Editors of the *Universities Quarterly* questioned whether this meritocracy would accept " ... a sense of social obligations and responsibilities". They observed that higher education would still be reserved for the few and that " ... the Newsom children will not, on the whole, become Robbins students".[5] They feared the proposals might make for an even more divisive society since " ... the social–cultural dichotomy between the higher educated and the less educated will inevitably be widened and the social consequences of this will not be trivial".[6] Reticence in exploring the social consequences of growing inequality was also at the root of the tension between advocacy of expansion and the maintenance of elite values which is the subject of the next section.

Expansion/elitism

The second analytical thread in the Robbins typology of objectives of higher education is the tension between expansion of student numbers on the one hand and the "transmission of a common culture and common standards of citizenship" on the other. The Report rejected any notion of a finite pool of ability and recommended that " ... courses of higher education should be available for all those who are qualified by ability and attainment to pursue them and who wish to do so" (CHE, p. 8). This strategy both legitimised the building of new universities which had already been initiated with central government funding and heralded an expansion in student numbers overall. Robbins's advocacy of limited expansion was clearly progressive but his values of a common culture and citizenship now appear to be conservative and elitist. The Report did indeed demonstrate with hard evidence that entry to university largely depended on the social class of the applicant. Its recommendations attempted to redress the exclusion of children from poorer families. Robbins, citing the need to introduce first generation students into higher education, argued that the ideal of equality of opportunity, if not equality itself, would be realised in part by isolating students from undesirable family influences:

> It is not merely by providing places for students from all classes that this ideal will be achieved but also by providing, in the atmosphere of the institutions in which students live and work, influences that in some measure compensate for any inequalities in home background. (p. 7)

As Bocock and Taylor point out " ... liberal education tends to be a system for the social reproduction of a governing elite" (2003, p. 230). Not surprisingly for Trow the CHE was "a liberal and expansionist document" but its "values were incompatible with mass higher education" (1989, p. 55).

Public funding/academic autonomy

The third dichotomy in the Report is the relationship between state funding and state regulation on the one hand and university autonomy and academic freedom on the other. The Report addressed the question of governance and made a number of recommendations, particularly in relation to the possible machinery of government for higher education. It commended the present system of maintaining an arm's length between the state and universities whereby the University Grants Committee (UGC) prevented continental style state control. This body, composed predominantly of academics, had been set up in 1919 under the aegis of the Treasury to advise on the disbursement of the government grant to universities. Robbins was conscious of the possible fragility of the current arrangement,

> We must make it clear ... that there is no absolute safeguard against interference with the distribution of grants to universities. It is a convention that the Government abstains. But it cannot bind its successors; nor is its own agreement likely to imply abstention in the face of major difficulties. (CHE, p. 237)

Robbins was sensitive to the question of the dilemma posed for the protection of university autonomy in the face of increasing dependence on state funding. The Report contained a detailed examination of academic freedom seen in its individual and institutional aspects. This covered freedom of appointments, freedom to determine curricula and standards, freedom of admissions, freedom to determine the balance between teaching and research and freedom to determine the shape of development. Robbins believed that " ... a system that aims at the maximum of independence compatible with the necessary degree of public control is good in itself, as reflecting the ultimate values of a free society" (p. 230).

One issue of considerable public law significance was the machinery of government which would both safeguard academic freedom and allow accountability for national expenditure. The Report applauded the superiority of the existing arrangements since:

> ... detailed scrutiny of the expenditure of particular institutions is incompatible with that free initiative and full responsibility that is in the national interest to preserve. Our travels abroad have convinced us more than ever of the immense value of the British system whereby detailed public justification of particular university expenditure is not required. (CHE, p. 244)

Scrutiny of university funding would assume greater importance since state funding through taxation was to increase. The Report optimistically expected that the economy would continue to expand and that

> ... this increase in cost would be accompanied by a more than proportionate increase in the gross national product; for the latter would grow, not only with the labour force, but at a further three and a quarter percent per annum as well. (CHE, p. 208)

The Report expressed confidence that citizens would be prepared to pay additional taxes to fund the expansion of higher education:

> ... it is not unreasonable to expect that the nation should be prepared spend a higher proportion [of national income] on services such as higher education. ... One may buy less of services such as bus travel if one's income rises, but surely not less of education. To spend more on higher education would almost certainly be the average family's individual response. Why should it not be assumed to be true of the community of families considered collectively? (p. 208)

The Report is clearly influenced by the consensus welfare state and public good assumptions which still prevailed in the 1960s. Whiggish optimism that the population would see higher education as a desirable object for their taxes was, however, taken for granted rather than argued in any sustained way. Robbins's LSE colleagues included the neo-liberal economist Hayek but also Marshall and Titmuss, leading sociologists and theorists of welfare.[7] Robbins, it seems, did not engage with their intellectual analysis of a citizenship based on systems of mutual support and a benign role for the state.[8] By contrast with these theorists, Robbins's programme for the expansion of higher education, with all that implied for state funding, appears overly defensive in its objectives for that specific aspect of the public sphere. The question of whether the state should have a role at the margins or the centre was a contested one because of the need to preserve academic freedom and autonomy. It is a limitation of the Report in that it concentrated largely on efficiency arguments for increasing public funding rather than addressing at a deeper theoretical level the desirable parameters of the state's overall relationship with higher education institutions. As Niblett observed, "Robbins could have thought out its own philosophy of higher education more compellingly, leaving it less implicit" (1981, p. 1).

For Carswell, under-secretary at the Office of the Lord President of the Council, it was the practical elements of the Robbins Report which were limited. He explained why colleagues should not describe it as a 'plan':

> The expression 'Robbins plan' is an unfortunate one. Beveridge was a plan to be implemented by the Government. Robbins is a set of objectives for the Government and the institutions to achieve and the ways of achieving it are left – as they must be in the nature of higher education – to those concerned to work out.[9]

Of course it was a reasonable assumption that leading insiders within government, the civil service and the universities would not contest the Robbins objectives. At the time there was a largely unspoken identity of outlook and a 'special relationship' between academics, politicians and senior civil servants. Scott observed (1988, p. 45):

> Key to this special relationship was that a community of interest between higher education and the state was taken for granted. Academic leaders and political and administrative leaders were all members of the same national elite. They shared the same silent allegiances to the same unarticulated values.

Such mutuality of interests, although for the most part unarticulated, was to undergo change later when the ideological ground shifted from the consensus on welfarism in the 1960s to the more controversial and openly expressed meta-narrative of the market, commencing globally in the 1980s.[10] However, even in the immediate decade following Robbins, senior civil servants expressed reservations about the Report's objectives. The next section demonstrates how departmental officials alighted on the implicit dichotomies in the Report, identified above, and gave somewhat limited endorsement to public good values in higher education.

Whitehall and Robbins

Utility/knowledge for its own sake

Tensions between economic and intellectual objectives for higher education were not new. In 1948 the Terms of Reference of the UGC had been amended to give it an additional aim,

> . . . and to assist, in consultation with the universities and other bodies concerned, the preparation and execution of such plans for the development of the universities as may from time to time be required in order to ensure that they are fully adequate to national needs.[11]

Tapper, however, suggests that in practice this amendment had little impact on the practice of the UGC. The UGC's main role was, he writes, to act as a "major defence of the liberal ideal of the university" (2007, p. 29). In 1963 senior civil servants still appeared to endorse this ideal. Evidence of the political enthusiasm for Robbins is to be found in the memorandum of John Boyd-Carpenter, Chief Secretary to the Treasury presented to Cabinet. He noted that implementing the Robbins recommendations " . . . would achieve remarkable social change in one decade". His concluded

> My colleagues will wish to have in mind the very heavy increase in public expenditure involved in acceptance of these recommendations . . . The basis of a decision to proceed with these proposals can only be a decision to give a definite measure of priority over other activities to this very large expansion in the provision of higher education.[12]

Shattock comments,

> It is obvious from the Treasury evidence to Robbins and the way this paper was couched in terms of social/cultural arguments that the idea of university expansion (almost certainly more than higher education expansion) ignited a latent idealism even in those charged with managing the nation's finances.

He points out that the projected expenditure was based on a growth rate of GNP assumed to be 4 per cent per annum and that Treasury officials " . . . must have recognised that the financial arrangements were a fudge which were bound to be unpicked and cause trouble at some future date" (2012, p. 141).

A more guarded view was expressed in a set of papers which had been prepared by Treasury officials, with assistance from Education Departments, the UGC and the Office of the Minister for Science, which Boyd Carpenter presented to the Ministerial Committee on Education Policy. This commented on the relationship between expanding higher education and stimulating the economy and claimed that any positive results from Robbins would only be apparent in the long-term:

> It is probably true that an investment on this scale in human capital brings a return to the national economy, although not necessarily as good or better than investment in 'lower' education and training of other kinds. But this

> return comes only in the very long-run – a much longer period to fructify than investment in factories or power stations or houses. A decision to accept Robbins is a decision to postpone material advance. It is no worse for that but we have to face it.[13]

Ministers considered the Robbins Report ideologically congenial in its flagging the need to consider instrumental as well as emancipatory justifications for higher education expansion. A discussion on financial support from industry for universities illustrates this. Secretary of State for Education Edward Boyle wrote to Chancellor of the Exchequer Reginald Maudling about tax concessions for donations to universities from industrialists. He noted:

> All told, most universities obtain about 90% of their income from public funds of one kind or another and it is generally agreed that this is an unhealthy state of affairs. One cannot fail to be impressed by the different pattern in the USA where tax law provides no excuse for business to hold back on benefactions ... A more liberal approach to the tax treatment of donations might result in the appreciable increase in the level of such donations.

Boyle concluded by citing Robbins as support for such an approach: "I need hardly add that any concession in this field could be justified by the emphasis by N.E.D.C. [National Economic Development Council] and by Robbins on the importance of higher education to economic growth".[14]

Civil servants also saw the significance of closer links with industry although there was some difference of emphasis between the DES on the one hand and the Treasury and Inland Revenue on the other. A Treasury Memorandum read: "It seems very probable that this advancement would be most economically productive if its direction is determined not by the universities alone, but by the universities in conjunction with outside interests, industry being the most important among them".[15] On the issue of tax concessions for donations Carswell, by then under-secretary at the Department of Education and Science, expressed the centrality of economic objectives to the Government. In a letter to his opposite number at the Inland Revenue he rejected the latter's argument against tax concessions that this would create an uncertain revenue stream and difficulties in expenditure plans. Such a view, claimed Carswell, " ... would permit the desirability of the universities receiving no money except from the Government so that the Government could make sure it was spent to the maximum possible utility". Carswell claimed that private benefactions provided "the jam" with the result that "we are in a position more effectively to insist on bread-and-butter only from the UGC". He continued:

> But the much more important point here is that through donations and benefactions from firms a closer lien will be established between universities and industry; and this is one of the prime objectives of the Government with regard to the economy and higher education.[16]

Others in the Treasury on the other hand agreed with the Inland Revenue that fiscal disadvantage could result from tax concessions for donations to universities:

> A further consideration is that, whereas public expenditure programmes are under some sort of control, an increase in a flow of funds brought about by a tax concession is under no control whatever. I think therefore that it is at least questionable whether it is better to increase the resources devoted to university education by giving a tax concession as compared with increasing public expenditure on universities.[17]

Discussing this point with the Treasury, Carswell again made it clear that there was an ideological as well as a financial issue at stake: "The issue is not merely a financial one. Direct benefaction by industry should be a valuable way of bringing universities closer to industry and securing developments in them that benefit the economy".[18]

The evidence from the archives indicates that although the Robbins Report had been somewhat imprecise on the relationship between higher education and the economy, its emphasis on economic objectives was welcome by officials particularly in the DES. However, limited attention was accorded to any consequential affect of these utilitarian arguments on liberal education values.

Expansion/elitism

In relation to expansion in numbers and the difficulties this might pose for maintaining elite standards, departmental officials also identified some potential tensions. Publicly the Macmillan government applauded the values of the Robbins Report and officials suggested the following notes for the Prime Minister's speech welcoming its publication:

> The relevance [of the Robbins Report] to the future of democracy will be even greater than the economic benefits. The future of free society largely depends on the number of trained and qualified minds available within it. Quite apart from this the universal availability of university education will be the greatest solvent of class differences.[19]

Carswell perhaps had a clearer grasp of the implications of the Report and what was meant by higher education. He pointed out,

> Robbins is about higher education, not universities. The Government's obligation to make courses available for all those who are qualified by ability and attainment to pursue them and who wish to do so is in terms of higher education, not university education. About half the places in higher education are outside the universities.[20]

Carswell was doubtful that the Robbins proposals would be "the greatest solvent of class differences". That thesis was " . . . open to attack that the proposals are not to make higher education universal but to make it available to those who can profit by it, and some might argue this would accentuate class differences".[21] Some

Ministers also were uneasy about extravagant claims for the Report in terms of social mobility. Quintin Hogg, Lord President of the Council and Minister for Science, in a memorandum to the Cabinet on raising the school leaving age, noted that:

> Some sections of public opinion contrast the Government's ready acceptance of the Robbins Report with our silence on Newsom. We are accused of neglecting the great mass of average children in the interests of the elite minority.[22]

Officials implied that some of the worthier objectives of Robbins were platitudes. An Interdepartmental Committee of Officials on Education Policy was set up in September 1963, before the Report was published. Clarke, Permanent Secretary at the Treasury, had prepared a summary of the principal recommendations of the forthcoming Report. The first item read: "Higher Education should be available, predominantly at public expense, to all those who desire it and are academically qualified to pursue it; plans for expansion should be made accordingly".[23] He prepared an additional lengthy commentary for the Chief Secretary to the Treasury expanding on his summary, noting that this " ... represents very much my own initial views, which will no doubt be modified later". Clarke commented that the first item on the list was " ... really an expression of goodwill, rather like saying that everybody who is ill ought to have first-class hospital accommodation available, or that one ought to be able to drive from London to Sheffield without getting into traffic jams".[24] The next section will indicate much of the concern about expansion of numbers centred on whether it was affordable, but the departmental papers demonstrate that there was also recognition of other considerations. In terms of the tension between expansion and elitism some argued that primary and secondary education might have a greater claim to public support than higher education. There was also a perception that the generosity of Robbins's egalitarian vision for the facilities of an expanded higher education system, while appropriate for the few, was too lavish for the many.

Public funding/academic autonomy

Not surprisingly it was the third set of somewhat contradictory objectives derived from the Robbins Report which aroused the most comment on the part of officials.

The Treasury expressed alarm at the over-optimistic estimates of costs. In his lengthy commentary on the Robbins proposals Clarke went on to express a number of reservations. He anticipated that, "There will undoubtedly be lots of jobs which are now done perfectly adequately by people who leave school at 17 which will in future employ graduates. This has its social merits, but is it a good use of public money?". He suggested that:

> The essential point here is that the figures in the Report are certainly too low, because they do not take into account the various improvements in standards which are recommended and which will almost certainly happen unless action is taken in the contrary sense.[25]

The political implications of implementing Robbins were also cause for concern. Cary at the Cabinet Office commented to Rab Butler, Deputy Prime Minister and First Secretary of State:

> If the programme is acceptable up to 1980 there are serious implications for the fields of expenditure. By 1980 the expansion recommended would double the proportion of the GNP devoted to higher education. The Robbins Committee argue that this is what people want. But the same might be said for housing, health, school education or roads.[26]

Related to the fiscal difficulties identified in funding the expanded higher education system, was the problem of establishing a more robust system of public accountability, an area where Robbins had proposed little change to the status quo. The issue was to come to a head in Wilson's Labour administration, 1964–1970. The Public Accounts Committee (PAC) conducted an examination of university accountability in 1966 and proposed greater parliamentary control. What ensued was a lengthy series of discussions involving departmental officials, the UGC and Crosland, Minister of Education. The administrative details of the proposals are complex but the central issue was the form any new system of parliamentary accountability should take. Crosland agreed that the PAC should now have a greater role in scrutinising UGC accounts but resisted the favoured DES proposal which would have involved a fuller parliamentary debate and legislation. Andrew, Permanent Secretary at the DES, pressed for a statutory public Commission to administer Government assistance to the Universities. This would have a special relationship to Parliament through a Select Committee on University Affairs.[27] Both the UGC and Crosland however favoured a different system which more closely resembled the status quo. Irrespective of the relative virtues of the proposals, the significant point about the stance Crosland took was that he was opposed to any wider debate about accountability at this time. Departmental officials commented on his reluctance. Crosland had written to Wilson setting out his objections to the DES's proposed arrangement:

> While it is conceivable that after running the gauntlet of public debate we should end up with more than a statutory version of the present arrangements plus a Select Committee, the need for legislation would require precise definition of the future relationships between the Commission, the universities, the Government and Parliament. Such a definition would be extremely difficult; and it would involve controversial debate both in Parliament and beyond about the exact status of universities and indeed the whole of our higher education policy. I do not think we want such a debate at this time ....

He was anxious about political repercussions if too radical a stance was adopted:

> While I have now firmly established, as part of our policy for higher education, a 'public sector' represented by the colleges of education and the polytechnics and other technical colleges, I have been accused within the Party of trying to preserve a privileged position for the universities. The

> creation of a statutory corporation to look after them, leaving the other colleges outside its purview, would open us to the charge that we wished to isolate the universities further from public influence.

His recommendation was for the arrangement which " ... minimises the risk of controversy in that in an uncertain situation it involves the least change from the present arrangements ... ".[28] Treasury officials were rather uneasy at this outcome. They noted that Crosland, " ... concerns himself almost entirely with avoiding controversy".[29]

Both in the Robbins Report itself and in the surrounding departmental discussions, the public good arguments for a state funded higher education system were made defensively. Crosland's reluctance to initiate a wider debate at a time when the institution of the polytechnics was bringing a new dimension to the concept of 'public' and to the vocational role of higher education provides a further illustration of this abstention. The pivotal role of the Department of Education and Science in rejecting Robbins's advocacy of a unified higher education system where all institutions might aspire to become universities (eventually) has been well documented. For Taylor and Steele, DES Permanent Secretary Weaver "set about dismantling the Robbins Report" in his determination to keep the polytechnics within the local authority aegis and was successful in persuading Crosland to execute this. They explain, "Crosland's policy stance was thus influenced by these two complementary arguments: the vested bureaucratic interests of the Ministry's Fabian officials; and the missionary, Labourite zeal of the activist professional staff of the technical colleges" (2011, p. 88). The evidence from the departmental papers is that Crosland was not prepared to base this policy decision on an exposition of an integrative or coherent set of principles. Arguably such a public debate would have given higher education a better intellectual framework for withstanding the neo-liberal agenda of the 1980s. Crosland appeared reluctant to sanction a wider debate at an early stage of the expansion of higher education at a time when there was a greater public appetite for funding it out of taxation. The absence of a strategy for mobilising popular support in the country more widely increased higher education's vulnerability to the neo-liberal policies which followed the election of a right-wing Conservative administration in 1979. One of the immediate objectives of that administration was to cut public spending and the universities were a prime target in the 1981 cuts which for Shattock " ... marked a policy divide in the history of higher education" (2012, p. 129). The ideological context of the policy changes in higher education in the 1980s is the subject of the last section of the article. Before turning to these, the article considers the impact of the discussions surrounding Robbins on the Ormrod Report on Legal Education, published in 1971.

The Ormrod Committee

Just four years after the publication of Robbins, Labour Lord Chancellor Gerald Gardiner set up a committee, chaired by Mr Justice Ormrod, to consider and make recommendations for developing legal education. Ormrod was much influenced by

Robbins's liberal philosophy and quoted from it in his own report (CLE, p. 46). Ormrod recommended that universities should play a much greater role in teaching law. The Report recommended that the traditional divide between the academic and vocational aspects of legal education "must be eliminated by adjustments on both sides" (p. 34). It proposed abandoning the existing position whereby the law degree gave graduates an exemption from parts of the professional examinations for aspiring barristers and solicitors. Instead the degree itself should be the qualification permitting the law graduate to proceed to the vocational training. The Ormrod Committee however left the implementation of the Report to another committee which was to be established for that purpose, namely the Lord Chancellor's Advisory Committee on Legal Education. As Cocks and Cownie put it, this committee was "very much a creature of the profession" (2009, p. 131). It was particularly concerned to exercise influence over the content of the law degree curriculum. Thus, while Ormrod had recommended that there should be five core subjects, the professional bodies successfully argued for the addition of trusts and for the inclusion of administrative law in the constitutional law curriculum. However, the influence of the legal profession on the direction of higher education ranged beyond the Advisory Committee. The archives reveal that it went some way to undermine Gardiner's wider reforming zeal.

The Lord Chancellor had initially high ambitions for the outcome of Ormrod. He wrote to Premier Wilson, "One advantage would I hope be the introduction into the curriculum of subjects such as criminology, penology, and the sociology of law, which have so far formed virtually no part of the lawyers' education".[30] His aspirations were not welcome to the legal establishment. A series of secret exchanges early in 1967 between Sir John Wolfenden, Chair of the UGC, and Lord Justice Diplock (who was appointed the next year Lord of Appeal in Ordinary) reveal the conservatism of the judiciary towards any such innovations. Wolfenden noted that Diplock had earlier informed him that "he was not interested in 'law as a liberal education' or 'law as an ingredient in courses for Probation Officers'. He was interested solely in recruitment to the profession, particularly of solicitors, for whom the demand was almost unlimited".[31] Diplock's vision of a law curriculum was decidedly narrow but Wolfenden was dependent on judicial support. He sought Diplock's assistance in convincing the new universities to teach law and noted, "I said we might well need advice on quinquennial proposals and [Diplock] said he would be willing to be consulted secretly and informally by me personally".[32] Such secret exercise of judicial power was one of a number of factors which made law schools particularly vulnerable to what Bradney refers to as a "call for a closer connection between the academic world and 'the world of work'" (2003, p. 73). Another factor was the inhibition of legal academics in championing the Ormrod Committee's proposal for the conclusive status of the law degree. Cownie and Cocks comment,

> The implications of legal academia's failure to secure the implementation of Ormrod's fundamental recommendation that the law degree should be recognised, without more, as enabling students to fulfil the academic stage of legal training continue to haunt successive generations of law teachers. (2009, p. 132)

Finally the vulnerability of liberal education values in law schools was increased by what some commentators identified as a theoretical weakness in the Ormrod Report as a whole. This argument is an echo of critical academic commentary on the Robbins Report for under-theorising the nature of the public good in higher education. Arthurs noted that Ormrod "did not take up the opportunity to articulate a public interest rationale for university based professional education" (1971, p. 643). Thomas and Mungham were critical of what they saw as Ormrod's conservatism and noted, "There is a strong suggestion of utility and practicality running throughout the Report which, rather than attempting to revolutionize, sets out to legitimize, update, harmonize and consolidate" (1972, p. 114). They feared that it was overly tolerant of the profession's social elitism and of its failure to embrace new areas such as welfare law. They wrote,

> To put it bluntly, the English legal system has succeeded in maintaining a professional establishment which, in terms of its size, training, social characteristics and services offered, differs only in detail from the legal profession which existed at the turn of the century. Little or nothing of this stasis comes through to the reader of the Ormrod Report. (p. 125)

Law, arguably more than other disciplines, had long demonstrated an intimate accommodation between liberal education and utilitarian values. Sugarman, in tracing the intellectual history of Anglo-American legal education, identified one of its components as the assumption

> that the professional training of lawyers for professional tasks (narrowly conceived as private law in character) was the primary goal of modern law schools; and that the standpoint of law teachers was that of elite lawyers and appellate judges, that is as 'insiders' of the legal system. (2011, p. 11)

The reach of appellate judges, as the case of Diplock demonstrates, included secret exchanges with other insiders such as the chair of the UGC. Of course there were contrary influences in play which eventually shaped the prevailing ideological landscape. These included the growing professional confidence of legal academics from the early 1970s, for example in establishing a flourishing culture of socio-legal studies. As Bradney points out (citing as an example the 1996 ACLEC Report[33]), "... there were also a number of reports and statements from outside the universities that supported the idea of a liberal education in university law schools". However he adds that

> it would be difficult to argue that these latter statements suggest a depth of support for liberal education in the legal professions that would be such as to indicate a willingness to voice significant opposition to government plans for university law schools. (2003, p. 73)

In the case of both the Robbins and Ormrod Reports the published rhetoric about liberal education values was accompanied by secret Whitehall arrangements which were not subject to open debate. Such avoidance of wider engagement about the changes needed in higher education in general and legal education in particular made the sector all the more exposed to the structural changes earmarked for the public services by the administration which took office in 1979.

Extending the 'product range': the advocacy of market values

The Thatcher government's objective for all public services was a smaller, stronger state accompanied by effective monitoring of institutional performance to ensure compliance. Higher education was not exempt. In September 1982 the Cabinet discussed proposals for radical reductions in public expenditure. A memorandum was presented by the Central Policy Review Staff (CPRS) the 'think tank' based in the Cabinet Office and composed of seconded civil servants and other 'advisors' from industry, commerce and universities. The memorandum suggested that "It may well be desirable to make higher education more market-oriented, giving more choice to consumers and making the system more responsive to the needs of both students and employers". One suggestion was for higher education institutions to receive no grant directly from government (except for research) and to be funded entirely through student fees, plus any outside endowment funds institutions could raise. Student loans were considered as another cost saving policy.[34] Thatcher, expressing concern about the "sensitivity of the subject", commissioned the CPRS to prepare a Report on 'The Responsiveness of Higher Education to Market Forces and Employment Needs'.[35] (The CPRS had produced a series of reports for Ministers often covering the work of several departments and concentrating on strategic aims.[36]) The final report of the committee on higher education was presented to the Prime Minister in July 1983.[37] Although few of its specific recommendations were implemented at the time the analysis it contains provides a rich source of neo-liberal thinking at an early stage of the Thatcherite reforms of public services. It also reveals that Thatcher personally took a keener interest in higher education than researchers had hitherto assumed.

The team preparing the Report was led by civil servant Gordon Wasserman who was the CPRS Head of Social Policy.[38] Comments on the various drafts give a clear indication of the new ideological vision now taking hold. Michael Elliott, a co-opted member, showed an awareness of the constitutional issues involved: "We do have a genuine and radical goal – that of transforming the nature of the contribution that higher education can make towards society".[39] Encouraging 'responsiveness' on the part of the higher education institutions was a desirable strategy since it " … avoids Bonapartist direction of what, in other countries, would be regarded, without controversy, as arms of the 'state'. It is good for the soul, and honest to the spirit of the constitution". However, he continued, "We can if we wish go further and say that if responsiveness does not bring change about, then we must try 'dirigisme'".[40]

The Robbins Report is not referred to directly in the final draft of the Report but many of the CPRS's objectives implicitly challenge it. The introduction to the CPRS Report made clear its difference of emphasis:

> We decided to focus on three main objectives of our higher education system, which we have called the economic, the academic and the educational. We began our work by examining the extent to which our present higher education arrangements meet each of these objectives.[41]

The Report considered that universities had placed undue emphasis on the academic objective and proposed ways of redressing the balance. It thus set fresh challenges to the dichotomies inherent in Robbins.

Utility/knowledge for its own sake

In both universities and in the public sector colleges, "relevance or usefulness", argued the Report, had been given too little weight since:

> ... over-riding concern for high academic standards ... has left other, less desirable, marks on our institutions of higher education. It has meant that when considering the value of a subject for study (either as research or by students) too little weight is given to relevance or usefulness to the outside world.[42]

The Report referred dismissively to a feature of the "university ethos" which held that

> academics must be free not only to determine their own academic interests but also determine their own conditions of employment, what courses are to be offered, how much research as opposed to teaching they should do and when they should do it.[43]

The solution proposed was that "the system must be more exposed to market forces and more able to react to them".[44] There was confidence that "the 'economic' objective [underlined in original] of higher education will become increasingly important".[45] Similarly the "educational objective" was described as one which focused "on the individual, not on the economy or on some abstract notion of knowledge for its own sake".[46]

Expansion/elitism

The Report's proposals for expansion in numbers of students were innovatory. It proposed that "Government should use the leverage of its funding to persuade institutions to open their doors to a more diverse student body by accepting a wider range of entry qualifications including qualifications in vocational education".[47] In listing how to attract applicants the Report adopted the language of commerce:

> To this end it needs to have a diverse product range (different courses), it needs to draw its raw material (intending students) from a range of backgrounds and it needs to be responsive to demands for its final products from a wide range of customers (society as a whole, the academic world, employers, individuals). It is likely that these needs will be met most effectively if there is considerable diversity of producers (higher education institutions).[48] [Words in brackets in the original]

Grants for part time study for working adults with families to support should be introduced although the Report did not propose that "adults should be given a statutory right to education leave, with or without pay from their employer. This would increase burdens on employers and could help to destroy jobs".[49] The educational objective "aims to help people lead fuller, richer lives and to play more effective roles in society".[50] However little was added to explain the content of this generalisation. The CPRS Report is less concerned than Robbins with the social induction of new groups of higher education applicants but more radical in its proposals for increasing the numbers and diversity of students and in anticipating the concept of life-long learning. Higher education institutions are pictured as resistant to making necessary changes and the Report is very critical of their current ethos, picturing it as rather a site of *Brideshead* nostalgia and elite discipline specialism:

> Our present system of higher education has become hallowed by generations of tradition, personal loyalty, memories and myths. There is thus tremendous inertia in it, further buttressed by the mutual reinforcing links which have been forged between it and the specialised school curriculum. Overcoming this inertia so as to be able to implement the changes necessary to make the system more responsive to changing needs will require far more than exhortation. It will require sustained, strong, pressure from the Government over many years.[51]

Public funding/academic autonomy

The Report stated that "We reject the idea that what is required is a significant increase in public spending on higher education" [underlining in original]. In part this was because the CPRS was not convinced that this would have had a direct impact on economic growth. There was " ... no clear evidence of a link between investment in higher education and economic performance" and it was " ... questionable therefore whether higher education should have first claim on any extra resources for raising the general educational attainment of the labour force". It was "at least as important to increase educational participation between 16 and 18 and among adults who have had no post-compulsory education". Changes could be achieved "within present public funding levels by increasing the effectiveness and efficiency of our system and by attracting more private finance".[52] "Our approach", proclaimed the Report, "is through the market". The Government's role was to " ... take steps to improve the flow and quality of information essential for any market to work effectively" and to " ... use the financial levers available to it more positively with a view to giving the institutions of higher education greater incentives to respond to the need to change". This could, it seems, be done without adversely affecting academic freedom. The proposals would:

> ... mean increasing the extent to which the Secretary of State is concerned with affairs of particular institutions, but we believe both that such an extension of his role is necessary in order to ensure that the Government's preferred balance between objectives is achieved and that is consistent with respecting the fundamental academic freedoms on which our system of higher education rests.[53]

Specific funding proposals included separating the block grant for each institution into research and teaching components and a phased introduction of student loans for fees and maintenance.

Sparrow, in presenting the Report to the Prime Minister, was sensitive to its controversial nature. He observed that "... premature indications of how the Government might want to react to new thinking in this area could conceivably provoke adverse reactions from the academic establishment".[54] Thatcher's private secretary noted that the Prime Minister agreed that a copy of the Report should be sent to the Secretary of State for Education and Science to consider its recommendations.[55] A more marketised approach was the basis of the 1988 Education Act with the new funding councils replacing the UGC.

Conclusion

The production and content of the CPRS Report suggests that, in the space of the two decades since Robbins, the ideology of the market in higher education had taken hold and could be put coherently and persuasively within Whitehall. This process was to gather apace in the succeeding decades. Economic stringency, an instrumental approach to knowledge and fostering individual ambition, gradually encroached on support for public funding, critical engagement with ideas and collegiality. The intellectual ground-work had been put in place for the new policies, although it would take another thirty years before they were fully implemented. The installation of the neoliberal project required first a protracted theoretical onslaught on the public domain. For the CPRS, public higher education institutions needed the discipline of the market. As Ward puts it, for ideologues like Thatcher, public bodies, including universities, "... were at best incentiveless, unproductive and wasteful systems that were drags on the expansion of markets or at worst destroyers of the moral self-reliance of people" (2012, p. 3).

The CPRS critique of higher education as predominantly an individual rather than a public service amounted to a rejection of traditional public good values implicitly if not explicitly. The rejection was to be all the more smoothly incorporated into official discourse because Whitehall, seizing upon some incoherences in Robbins, had already conceded only muted support for these. The outcome produced somewhat of an ideological mixed bag. As Kogan and Hanney observed, "So far from enforcing single ideologies upon higher education, government, perhaps through avoidance of fundamental reappraisals, seems to be content to allow several ideologies and principles and practices to run in parallel" (2000, p. 224). It seems that the academy itself also draws back from championing the public role of higher education. As Calhoun observed,

> ... one of the problems faced by universities is the generally weak articulation of the nature and rationale for public expenditure and public governance in pursuit of public goods – a problem that extends well beyond universities (though one might think they have an interest in addressing it. (2006, p. 12)

Such defensiveness is not unique to higher education. Harris, Beveridge's biographer, argues that the welfare state " ... came into being with no clearly defined perception of welfare and no coherent theory of the state" (1987, p. 257). Furthermore, today's theorists of the need for increased state intervention to achieve a fairer society, on Keynesian or social democratic grounds, infrequently refer to higher education.[56] The above account has demonstrated that a multiplicity of values, perhaps healthily so, has long characterised discussion of higher education at least since the Robbins Report. Ambiguities in Robbins and in Ormrod allowed the exposition of utilitarian justifications for higher education, including legal education, to overshadow all others, culminating in the 1983 CPRS Report. Revelation of the existence of the Report is significant for higher education researchers not so much because it heralded immediate policy implementation but because it provides additional evidence for the proposition that Thatcher's marketisation crusade, subsequently embraced by Major, by New Labour and by the Coalition, was from the outset a totalising and a long-term project, from which no institutions, however venerable, escaped.[57]

Ward, reviewing the history of the inroads of neo-liberalism in higher education, argues that we need to " ... recognise these outcomes as the result of human intentionality created through political and social action rather than being abstractions of something called 'the economy' or 'globalisation'" (2012, p. 10). Given that the assertion of market values in higher education was driven by ideology rather than economic imperative, then arguably it is incumbent on those who resist such a project to be equally robust in upholding public good and collectivist values. There is a need for advocacy of more intellectually coherent alternative paradigms both within and without the academy than has hitherto been the case. Law academics are facing the specific challenge of LETR. As Guth and Ashford explain,

> Nothing in the LETR precludes a liberal education and nothing in it suggests socio-legal studies have no place, but the report has the potential to be taken as a starting point for regulation of UG degrees which is based on an incomplete picture.

They call for other voices, as well as those centred on vocationalism, to be heard (2014, p. 19). Current controversies about such matters as funding, governance, research focus, teaching methods and managerialism provide new spaces for such discussions. As Zeldin reassuringly observes, " ... there is now unprecedented disagreement about what universities are for. That has advantages. It discourages mere imitation of traditional patterns and justifies experimentation" (2014, p. xi).

Acknowledgements

I am grateful for comments from Professor Michael Shattock, Institute of Education, on earlier drafts of the paper and for the helpful comments of the anonymous reviewers. Participants in the discussions at the Hart Workshop on Legal Education, Institute of Advanced Legal Studies, June 2014 and at the Annual Conference of the Society for Research into Higher Education, December 2014, also gave much valued feedback on earlier drafts. Responsibility for any remaining errors is mine.

Disclosure statement

No potential conflict of interest was reported by the author.

Notes

[1] Williams refers to the 'Tawney principle' which held that " ... what good parents want for their children a good state should provide for all its children". He comments, "After the Robbins Report (1963) advocated higher education expansion it was implicitly assumed that the principle could be extended to include academic education of young adults, as it is explicitly in several European countries" (2011, p. 1).

[2] For the effect of privatisation on law schools see Thornton (2012).

[3] T.N.A. CAB 184/715, 'Responsiveness of Higher Education to Market Forces and Employment Needs', 1983.

[4] See 'The Perspectives of Robbins', Editorial (December 1963) 18(1) *Universities Quarterly* 7.

[5] Ibid. In 1961 David Eccles, Education Secretary, commissioned the Central Advisory Committee to produce a report on the educational provision for children who had failed the eleven-plus selection test and attended secondary modern schools. The Committee was chaired by John Newsom and its Report, *Half our Future*, was published in 1963.

[6] Ibid.

[7] See Marshall (1950) and Titmuss (1958).

[8] Freeden (2003, p. 290) contrasts Marshall with the ideology of the "post-Thatcherite age" where rights are "reduced to a conditional status" and "their attainment is to all effects and purposes commercialised".

[9] T.N.A. ED 188/12, Carswell, 1 November 1963.

[10] One recent study of public administration has identified a "politicisation of the UK civil service" from the 1980s onwards, see Brown (2014, p. 116).

[11] Quoted in Shattock (2012, p. 14).

[12] T.N.A. CAB 129/114, Memorandum by the Chief Secretary to the Treasury and Paymaster General, 1 October 1963.

[13] T.N.A. ED 188/10, Memorandum by the Chief Secretary to the Treasury and Paymaster General, 24 September 1963.

[14] T.N.A. T 227/1394, Boyle to Maudling, 11 August 1964.

[15] T.N.A. T 227/1394, Bennett to Hancock, 18 August 1964.

[16] T.N.A. T 227/1394, Carswell to Harrison, 26 January 1965.

[17] T.N.A. T 227/1394, Hancock to Bennett, 27 August 1964.

[18] T.N.A. T 227/1394, Carswell, 8 January 1965.

[19] T.N.A. ED 188/12, suggested points on the Robbins Report for inclusion in the Prime Minister's speech, 1 November 1963.

[20] T.N.A. ED 188/12, Carswell to Burrett, 1 November 1963.

[21] Ibid.

[22] T.N.A. CAB 129/116, The School Leaving Age. Memorandum by the Lord President of the Council and Minister for Science, 2 January 1964. See also note 5.

[23] T.N.A. CAB 134/1667 E 63(5), Note by R.W.B. Clarke, 12 September 1963.

[24] T.N.A. T 325/94, The Robbins Report, R.W.B. Clarke, 13 September 1963.

[25] Ibid.

[26] T.N.A. CAB 21/5532, The Robbins Report, Cary to Secretary of State, 17 September 1963.

[27] T.N.A. T 227/2519, Draft Minute, April 1967.

[28] T.N.A. T 227/2519, Crosland to Wilson, 26 June 1967.

[29] T.N.A. T 227/2519, Rampton to Bell, 30 June 1967.

[30] T.N.A. PREM 13/1697, Gardiner to Wilson, 23 November 1967.

[31] T.N.A. UGC 7/1239, Wolfenden, 3 February 1967.

[32] Ibid.
[33] *The Fist Report on Legal Education and Training*, Lord Chancellor's Advisory Committee on Legal Education and Conduct, 1996, (ACLEC, 1996. p. 57).
[34] T.N.A. CAB 129/215/6, Central Policy Review Staff, Memorandum to Cabinet, Longer Term Options, Annex H, 6 September 1982. See Hillman (2013) for a history of the debates on student loans.
[35] T.N.A. CAB 164/1687, Sparrow to Joseph, 19 October 1982.
[36] The Report on Higher Education was one of the last it was to produce since the CPRS was disbanded in June 1983, in part because of Thatcher's irritation that the content of a number of them (although not the Report on Higher Education) had been leaked. James comments: "Mrs Thatcher's conversion of the Staff into an increasingly partisan body made it more and more controversial" (1986, p. 423).
[37] T.N.A. CAB 184/715, Responsiveness of Higher Education, 23 July 1983.
[38] As Lord Wasserman, he was made a Conservative peer and was Coalition advisor on policing and criminal justice.
[39] T.N.A. CAB 184/714, Elliott to Wasserman, 16 May 1983.
[40] Ibid.
[41] T.N.A. CAB 184/715, Higher Education Report by the Central Policy Review Staff, July 1983, p. 1.
[42] Ibid., p. 8.
[43] Ibid., p. 9.
[44] Ibid., p. 1.
[45] Ibid., p. 10.
[46] Ibid., p. 11.
[47] Ibid., p. 26.
[48] Ibid., p. 14.
[49] Ibid., p. 28.
[50] Ibid., p. 11.
[51] Ibid., p. 39.
[52] Ibid., p. 14.
[53] Ibid., p. 14.
[54] T.N.A. CAB 184/715, Sparrow to Prime Minister, 21 July 1983.
[55] T.N.A. CAB 184/715, Fleshner, 25 July 1983.
[56] For example Judt (2010) and Mazzucato (2013).
[57] Taylor and Steele comment that, " . . . Labour has adopted a Thatcherite, neo-liberal perspective, albeit cloaked in Third Way rhetoric" (2011, p. 2).

References

i) Unpublished sources

Government papers in The National Archives, Kew (T.N.A.)

CAB – Cabinet Office series

ED – Department Education series

PREM – Prime Minister's Private Office Papers.

T – Treasury series

ii) Published sources

Arthurs, H. (1971) The Ormrod report: a Canadian reaction, *Modern Law Review*, 34, pp. 642–654.

Bocock, J. & Taylor, R. (2003) The labour party and higher education: the nature of the relationship, *Higher Education Quarterly*, 57(3), pp. 220–238.

Bradney, A. (2003) *Conversations, Choices and Chances* (Oxford, Hart).

Brown, C. (2014) *Making Evidence Matter. A New Perspective for Evidence-Informed Policy Making in Education* (London, Institute of Education Press).

Calhoun, C. (2006) The university and the public good, *Thesis Eleven* 84(1) pp. 7–43.

Committee on Higher Education. (1963) Lord Robbins, Chairman, Cmnd 2154.

Committee on Legal Education. (1971) Hon Mr Justice Ormrod, Chairman, Cmnd 4595.

Cownie, F. & Cocks, R. (2009) *A Great and Noble Occupation!* (Oxford, Hart).

Freeden, M. (2003) Citizenship and civil society, in: J. Harris, (Ed) *Civil Society in British History.* (Oxford, Oxford University Press), pp. 275–292.

Guth, J. & Ashford, C. (2014) The legal education and training review: Regulating socio-legal and liberal education? *The Law Teacher*, 48(1), pp. 5–19.

Harris, J. (1987) Political ideas and the debate on state welfare, in: J. Harris (Ed), *War and Social Change in British Society in the Second World War* (Manchester, Manchester University Press), pp. 63–187.

Hillman, N. (2013) From grants for all to loans for all: undergraduate finance from the implementation of the Anderson report (1962) to the implementation of the Browne report (2012), *Contemporary British History*, 27(3), pp. 249–270.

Howson, S. (2011) *Lionel Robbins* (Cambridge, Cambridge University Press).

James, S. (1986) The *central policy review staff*, 1970–1983, *Political Studies*, 34(3), pp. 423–440.

Judt, T. (2010) *Ill Fares the Land* (London, Allen Lane/Penguin).

Kogan, M. & Hanney, S. (2000) *Reforming Higher Education* (London, Jessica Kingsley).

Marshall, T.H. (1950) *Citizenship and Social Class* (Cambridge, Cambridge University Press).

Mazzucato, M. (2013) *The Entrepreneurial State. Debunking Public vs Private Sector Myths* (London, Anthem Press).

Niblett, R. (1981) Robbins revisited, *Studies in Higher Education*, 6(1), pp. 1–12.

Scott, P. (1988) Blueprint, or blue remembered hills? The relevance of the Robbins report to the present reforms of higher education, *Oxford Review of Education* 14(1), pp. 33–48.

Shattock, M. (2012) *Making Policy in British Higher Education 1945–2011* (Maidenhead, UK, Open University Press).

Sugarman, D. (2011) A special relationship? American influences on English legal education, c1870–1965, *International Journal of the Legal Profession*, 18(1–2) pp. 7–57.

Tapper, T. (2007) *The Governance of British Higher Education. The Struggle for Policy Control* (Dordrecht, Springer).

Taylor, R. & Steele, T. (2011) *British Labour and Higher Education 1945–2000* (London, Continuum).

Thomas, P. & Mungham, G. (1972) English legal education: a commentary on the Ormrod report, *Valparaiso University Law Review*, 7(1), pp. 87–132.

Thornton, M. (2012) *Privatising the Public University. The Case of Law* (London, Routledge).

Titmuss, R.H. (1958) *Essays on the Welfare State* (London, Allen and Unwin).

Trow, M. (1989) The Robbins trap: British attitudes and the limits of expansion, *Higher Education Quarterly*, 43(1), pp. 55–75.

Twining, W. (2014) LETR: the role of academics in legal education and training: 10 theses, *The Law Teacher*, 48(1), pp. 94–103.

Ward, S. (2012) *Neoliberalism and the Global Restructuring of Knowledge and Education* (London, Routledge).

Willetts, D. (2013) *Robbins Revisited. Bigger and Better Higher Education* (London, Social Market Foundation).

Williams, G. (2011) Some thoughts on higher education, Browne and Coalition policy, *London Review of Education*, 9(1), pp. 1–4.

Zeldin, T. (2014) Forward, in: Watson (Ed) *The Question of Conscience. Higher Education and Personal Responsibility* (London, Institute of Education Press), pp. x–xiii.

Legal education, ethics and access to justice: forging warriors for justice in a neo-liberal world

DONALD NICOLSON
School of Law, University of Strathclyde, Glasgow, UK

ABSTRACT *This article explores the reasons for a greater emphasis on access to justice in UK legal education and how law schools might go about raising awareness of the issue in students and fostering a commitment on their part to play a role in redressing problems of unmet legal need. It argues that the most effective means of doing so is through law clinics and other forms of voluntary legal services which expose students to the issue of unmet legal need and which may inspire them to seek to enhance access to justice when in practice. Moreover, it argues that the potential for the practical engagement by students with problems of access to justice is enhanced by the very same neo-liberal forces that make the issue of access to justice so urgent in UK society and which seem to militate against an education in which access to justice plays a central role.*

Introduction

One issue which has yet to receive any attention in the debate over the future shape of UK legal education post-LETR[1] is the place of access to justice (ATJ) in the curriculum. Currently, ATJ is one of eleven specified elements of one of six areas of required knowledge for Scottish qualifying law degrees (Law Society of Scotland, 2010), whereas the English and Welsh *Joint Statement on the Academic Stage of Training* (Law Society and the General Council of the Bar, 1995) ignores the topic altogether. Short of a survey, it is difficult to ascertain how many law schools buck the traditional focus on covering the professionally required core in great detail and providing substantive law options, but it is instructive that in the last survey of UK law schools (Harris & Beinart, 2004), only 20% taught legal system or skills courses, which along with brief, often unassessed, introductions to law constitute the traditional home for ATJ. No doubt, some academics might discuss ATJ in classes dealing with legal process, sociology of the law, etc., but clearly the topic has a precarious and peripheral place in the curriculum.

This article argues that ATJ should be a central concern for both legal education and legal practitioners, and explores the potential for inculcating such a concern in law graduates through both traditional courses and clinical experience. Indeed, it argues that this potential is enhanced by the very same neo-liberal forces that make the issue of ATJ so urgent in UK society today and which seem to militate against an education which prioritises the sort of critical, contextual and socio-legal approach which one might associate with ATJ teaching. To understand the paradox, it is necessary to start with these neo-liberal forces.

Access to justice and legal education in a neo-liberal world

In its contemporary (but not original) usage (Boas & Gans-Morse, 2009), neo-liberalism refers to an extreme form of laissez faire economic theory associated with Hayek and Friedman (see e.g. Clarke, 2004; Harvey, 2005; Thornton, 2010, Ch. 1). It champions economic liberalisation, privatisation, free trade and deregulated markets, and seeks to reduce government spending as far as possible. Neo-liberalists believe that leaving matters to private enterprise is far more efficient than collective action, and consequently seek to replace the state with private enterprise, and notions of social justice and the public good with profit-making and self-interest. As Sarat and Scheingold put it: "[w]hereas once laissez-faire meant keeping the state out of the market, today neoliberalism means bringing the market into the state" (Sarat & Scheingold, 2001, p. 7). In practice, virtually no sphere of UK society has been spared the neo-liberal turn – certainly not ATJ and higher education. Indeed, it has been said that neo-liberalism "has become incorporated into the commonsense way many of us interpret, live, and understand the world" (Harvey, 2005, p. 3), producing an intensively individualistic subject – *homo œconomicus* – who sees the world in terms of rational self-interest (see e.g. Read, 2009).

As regards the ATJ sphere, whether solely due to neo-liberal ideological imperatives or also rooted in more legitimate concerns for 'efficiency' and 'value for money', there has been a steady decline in legal aid funding and in the types of legal issues funded, and the subjection of legal aid lawyers to greater bureaucratic control through audit and the discipline of market mechanisms such as franchising and contracting (see e.g. Sommerlad, 1999, 2008; Paterson, 2011, Ch. 3). This has created both disincentives to practise legal aid law and incentives to routinise and depersonalise services to ensure profitability. But whatever the motivations and justifications for these developments, the result is an increase in obstacles to ATJ. These obstacles can be absolute – legal subjects lack assistance from a legal expert or the ability to understand and engage with the law themselves (see e.g. Genn, 1999; Genn & Paterson, 2001) – or relative – while they can engage with law, they suffer disadvantages in doing so compared to others, particularly legal opponents, because of their own inadequate legal knowledge and skills or because they receive inferior legal services (see e.g. Baldwin & McConville, 1977; Genn, 1987; Davis *et al.*, 1994; McConville *et al.*, 1994).

The impact of neo-liberalism on legal education has been most comprehensively documented by Thornton (e.g. 2010, 2012; see also e.g. Webb, 1999; Goldsmith, 2002; Bradney, 2003; Boon & Webb, 2010; Goldsmith & Bamford, 2010). Higher education in general has seen state investment plummet while student numbers shoot up, leading to increased teaching and administrative loads, and increased pressure to produce more research and more funded research. Moreover, especially after fees were introduced in England and Wales, a university education has been transformed from a public good into a commodity marketed to student 'consumers' who, in classical *homo œconomicus* terms, seem more interested in gaining credentials to compete on the labour market than intellectual and personal growth.

This is a familiar story for all academics, but law schools face additional pressures. One source is the legal profession, itself facing the chill winds of neo-liberalism in the form of cutbacks to legal aid and competition from outside providers following deregulation of legal services and the shrinking of traditional monopolies. Along with globalisation, this has led to law firms becoming bigger, and more profit-oriented and business minded (see e.g. Lee, 1992; Sommerlad, 1995; Francis, 2005). Consequently, they seek graduates with the necessary skills and knowledge to be practice-ready profit-makers. In fact, the demands of all law employers for skills training and from the powerful large law firms for a focus on legal subjects relevant to commercial practice are echoed within the academy. As consumers of education services burdened with debt, students demand that their education makes them attractive to those employers who can ensure that they can repay their debts as quickly as possible, thus increasing the pull of commercial law practice. The resultant enhancement of student credentialism means that many law students are only interested in taking the core doctrinal subjects and optional subjects perceived to be attractive to prospective employers, such as those involving skills training or which have the same property and profits orientation as the core. This vocational focus is echoed by university management which has an interest in maximising student employment in order to attract new customers and appease the god of university league tables [see Hazelkorn (2008) generally and Sauder and Espeland (2009) in relation to (US) law schools].

These pressures are not, however, uniformly felt. Elite universities are better placed than others to resist demands for greater vocationalism because students are arguably more interested in the cachet of their 'brand name' than subjects taught and many employers seem more interested in 'input' as represented by the new proxies for social class – school attended, school results and, most determinatively, the status of university attended – and only in 'output' as represented by a 'decent degree' (Sommerlad, 2007; Boon & Whyte, 2010, pp. 213, 220; Ashley & Empson, 2013). It is thus unsurprising that the 'new' universities have been more willing to produce vocationally-oriented curricula (Boon & Webb, 2010, p. 82). Nor has the neo-liberal project of constructing a hegemonic *homo œconomicus* subjectivity been entirely successful. Thus, some students still enter law school with altruistic rather than self-interested reasons for studying law (Nicolson, 2013, pp. 41–43).

Nevertheless, all law schools have undoubtedly changed from the days in which academics could teach according to their academic and political beliefs, albeit within the confines of qualifying degree requirements. Thornton is most exercised by the strangling of more theoretical, critical and social-legal approaches to law shortly after their birth in the 1970s. This reversal of such a 'socially liberal' legal education has, she argues, been accelerated by a number of cost-cutting measures like the reversion from small-group teaching to lectures which, like virtual and intensive learning, involve a 'one-way flow' of 'frozen knowledge' concentrating on doctrine, and from extended essays to unreflective forms of assessment like tests and hypothetical problems. However, while Thornton makes an eloquent call for law schools "to resist the temptation to produce narrow technocrats" (2012, p. 276), she offers little by way of concrete strategy for doing so.

Apart from Bradney's suggestion that the "ivory tower is better defended from behind a moat with a raised drawbridge" (1995; see also Bradney, 2003), a similar lack of strategy is displayed by those who champion the more traditional conception of a liberal education in which knowledge is regarded as an end in itself, students are educated as persons and not workers, and universities prepare graduates for citizenship as much as a career (e.g. Brownsword, 1999; Guth & Ashford, 2014). Bradney argues that a liberal legal education involves introducing law students to "a variety of conversations which are going on within law" (2003, p. 87) and to the all-pervasive nature of values in law, but without seeking to indoctrinate particular views. He accepts that wholly technical matters can and indeed should be taught; otherwise, the discussion of underlying legal principles and values will be shallow. However, he argues that "employers cannot expect university law schools to make sure that they get only those graduates who they find to be suitable employees" (2003, p. 172), not least because there is no common set of skills and knowledge in today's highly fragmented legal profession and because so many graduates do not enter practice.

By contrast, while also decrying the neo-liberal turn in legal education, Boon and Webb (2010) warn that ignoring professional demands for a greater vocational focus risks a university law degree being replaced as the primary route to professional qualification by alternatives such as private legal education. In such circumstances, the scope for more critical, theoretical and contextual approaches to law would dwindle to near vanishing point. Similarly, Goldsmith and Bamford (2010) and Boon and Whyte (2010) argue that students have an equally legitimate claim to be stakeholders in legal education, since without them law schools would not exist. According to Goldsmith and Bamford, "[w]ho we are as legal academics cannot be separated wholly from who our students are" (2010, p. 179) and thus law schools cannot ignore their demands for greater engagement with legal practice. However, they do not see such engagement in purely vocational or technocratic terms. Instead, it may provide opportunities for connecting the "aspirations of law students with professional ideals (justice, service, fairness) and the goals of a university-based education" (2010, p. 163; see also Goldsmith, 1999, 2002; Boon, 1998, p. 166). Moreover, according to Goldsmith (2002) and many others [see references cited by Nicolson (2008, p. 165, n. 120)], student involvement in live-client clinics provides the best means to this end, while also ensuring an appreciation of law, justice and legal ethics that cannot be gleaned from any amount of traditional legal education.

In the rest of the article, I apply these insights to the more specific goals of giving greater prominence to ATJ in legal education and inculcating in students a commitment to the ideal of community service. However, in doing so I will draw upon a law clinic model which differs to that envisaged by Goldsmith in providing, I will argue, a more propitious site for launching a counter-hegemonic challenge to the neo-liberal vision of legal practice. First, however, the case for law schools and law graduates to take ATJ more seriously needs to be made.

Taking access to justice seriously

Here, at least four reasons can be offered. The first and most obvious is that justice is a central concern of a liberal legal education in its traditional or more critical incarnations. And, if one is interested in justice, then one needs to highlight the fact that so many people are absolutely excluded from obtaining legal services or are handicapped by inferior legal services or self-representation in obtaining whatever substantive justice law offers. Indeed some argue that access to a lawyer is a human right (Luban, 2014) or at least an essential prerequisite for human dignity, the rule of law and law's legitimacy and possibly even democracy (Luban, 1988, Ch. 11, 2005).

Secondly, even if one's aim is simply to describe law in realistic (as opposed to black-letter) terms, it also seems necessary to pay due attention to the fact that so many people are unable to vindicate their rights or defend themselves against legal detriments. For instance, to teach employment law without mentioning the difficulties of obtaining legal aid or the impact of recent Employment Tribunal fees would be grossly misleading. Moreover, attention to ATJ helps illuminate the contours of substantive law. For example, areas of law dominated by case law will tend to reflect the interests of those who can access the courts and effectively vindicate their interests, rather than of those who cannot litigate or litigate effectively.

Thirdly, ATJ can be said to be highly relevant to legal education if, as is becoming increasingly the case (Webb *et al.*, 2013, pp. 4.65–4.67), one regards legal ethics as a core element of undergraduate legal education. This is because, by analogy with Rawls's argument that "[j]ustice is the first virtue of social institutions" (Rawls, 1999, p. 3), it can be argued that the first virtue of the ethical lawyer is to ensure ATJ. Traditionally, legal ethics discourse focuses on issues of the morality of representation, both from the internal dimension of how lawyers should treat clients – do they respect their autonomy, protect their secrets and zealously pursue their interests? – and the external dimension of how they should treat others affected by client representation – do they unjustifiably harm others, the administration of justice or the public interest more broadly? Such a focus, however, only goes so far in aligning lawyers' ethics with their calling to seek justice, which after all is the legitimatory justification for lawyers' professional status (Nicolson, 2013).

For one thing, the goal of making practitioners aware of the ethical dimension to legal representation is undermined where their scope for moral manoeuvre is highly constrained by financial considerations which cast morality as an unaffordable luxury or where responsibility for ethics tends to fall into the cracks because of the increasing specialisation of legal work or completely out of sight because of its increasing routinisation (see Nicolson & Webb, 1999, Ch. 3). This does not mean that law schools should not seek to ensure that law graduates enter practice with a desire to uphold ethical values where they can. However, it seems obvious that lawyers either devoting their career to those most in need of legal services or doing so pro bono is an improvement on them only providing ethically aware services to the shrinking group of those who can afford to pay or obtain legal aid.

Indeed, as I have recently argued (Nicolson, 2013), notions of reciprocity or gratitude towards the community, which through its taxes pays for school education and, still in Scotland, for much of the cost of legal education, suggest that lawyers have a moral obligation to help redress ATJ obstacles. Public investment in their education enables law students to enjoy substantial financial rewards, yet only those fortunate enough to afford lawyers or qualify for legal aid benefit from this investment. Moreover, a major obstacle to ATJ is the high fees charged by lawyers. Consequently, it can be argued that these lawyers have a moral duty to contribute in some way to repaying those who helped put them in their privileged position, but who do not benefit from this investment. Two further arguments support a moral obligation on lawyers to enhance ATJ. One is that their earnings are partly – albeit decreasingly – protected by state limitations on who can practise law and access legal processes. Secondly, many ATJ problems, especially of a relative nature, stem from often unnecessary and difficult to understand legal complexities created by lawyers serving their clients (and indirectly themselves by making legal assistance more necessary). Here, lawyers can be said to have a moral obligation to help remedy the resultant ATJ obstacles.

Indeed, and as a fourth reason for making ATJ more central to legal education, given that their livelihood is partly dependent on educating those who make a good living from legal practice, it is arguable that academics have a similar obligation to enhance ATJ through consistently emphasising ATJ in their teaching and/or researching issues of ATJ, but, preferably, because of the positive example it sets to students, through community legal work (Rhode, 2004, p. 157; Nicolson, 2012), as was relatively common in the past (Partington, 1988, p. 381).

Locating access to justice in the curriculum

If these arguments about taking the importance of ATJ in legal education are persuasive, they raise the question of its location in the curriculum and how we might inspire students to take ATJ seriously. I will concentrate largely on the latter issue since my views on the former largely track those I have previously expressed on teaching ethics at the academic stage of legal education, namely that this should be done both pervasively and in compulsory stand-alone classes, and then backed up through live-client clinical experience (Nicolson, 2008). While pervasive teaching will expose students to the ubiquitous nature of ATJ obstacles and how the law taught in the rest of the curriculum actually operates in practice, unless taught voluntarily, academics are likely to surreptitiously (or perhaps not so surreptitiously) undermine the intended message and hence necessitate a stand-alone class.

However, unlike legal ethics, this need not be a full class. Instead, there are many potential homes for discussing ATJ. In addition to its common location in Introduction to Law, Legal System and Legal Process classes, it could be taught alongside Legal Ethics or in Sociology of Law/Socio-Legal Studies classes. In addition to providing a comprehensive picture of the ATJ landscape, it is important that such classes are given a coherence, for instance by linking ATJ to related issues like the role of lawyers, legal ethics and legal professionalism, rather than comprising a ragtag of issues which come across as 'stuff not covered elsewhere in the important part of the curriculum'.

The more challenging issue involves the timing of stand-alone ATJ teaching. On the one hand, an early introduction to ATJ problems allows them to be referred to pervasively. It might also help prevent an indelibly rosy picture of law's justice developing and encourage a more critical approach generally. On the other hand, if ATJ is not taught pervasively there is a case for locating it towards the end of the degree. This will allow reference to examples from other classes of how ATJ problems undermine law and justice. Moreover, it is arguable that this will have more impact than if students are initially told: 'you are about to study areas of law which may provide valuable legal rights, but be aware that many people may not be able to access these rights', and then left to work out when and to what extent this applies. The impact of such a message is also likely to be undermined by the fact that incoming students expect to learn criminal law, contract, property law, etc. and may either pay less attention to non-substantive subjects or positively resent being distracted from 'real' law.

Access to justice and active learning

While ascertaining the most effective location for ATJ teaching is a matter of speculation, by contrast, and by analogy with the growing consensus around ethics teaching (see Nicolson, 2008, p. 165), few are likely to doubt that the most promising means of encouraging students to take ATJ seriously is through exposure to those most in need of legal services via university law clinics or placements ('externships' in US terminology) in external legal service agencies. Lectures and even the most imaginative small-group exercises, such as requiring students to decide how to allocate scarce legal aid resources amongst a list of needy applicants (victims of domestic abuse, asylum seekers, sacked single parents, etc.), are never going to compete with the well-recognised advantages of combining exposure to 'theoretical' knowledge with actual experience (see e.g. Bloch, 1982; Brayne *et al.*, 1998). Thus, learning in adults is more effective if it draws upon actual experiences, and if knowledge can be applied immediately in the fulfilment of expected future roles rather than stored for future use. Such learning also goes deeper – both in the sense of knowledge being better understood and more readily accessible – where learners are not treated as passive receptacles of abstract information to be memorised and regurgitated, but required to obtain and transform knowledge through self-discovery and reflection.

If evidence of these advantages of experiential (or active) learning in relation to ATJ is required, it can be seen in the spontaneous comments in both oral examinations and reflective diaries[2] by University of Strathclyde Law Clinic (USLC) student volunteers who either opt to take Ethics and Justice, a class exploring issues of legal ethics and ATJ in the context of their clinic cases, or are required to as part of the Clinical LLB which integrates clinic training and case experience into the standard LLB (see Nicolson, 2013, pp. 51–55). Thus, as one student responded in an oral examination when questioned about what she had most learnt from four years of clinic experience: "Theoretically in Legal Process [a first year class] they tell you that there is an unmet legal need, but that is one of those things that are intangible unless you really experience it". In answer to the same question, another said:

> ... the system is mince. You don't realise how bad it is in the abstract, reading tables about legal aid. And then you realise that it is endemic and desperate, and it's only getting worse. The amazing thing is that it is so pervasive that it has come up in every essay I have written this year.

Similar views were expressed in a diary entry:

> Before I joined the Clinic I had a strong, but quite vague, feeling that there was injustice in the legal system, but now having been involved with clients and cases I feel that I have a much more focused idea of what the problems are and where the injustice comes from, especially the availability (or lack thereof) of Legal Aid funding and the way the Tribunal system runs compared to how it was supposedly designed to ....

Nevertheless, it is one thing for students to appreciate the extent of ATJ problems and quite another for them to take remedial action once they graduate. Adapting Rest's now familiar model of the four psychological conditions required for moral behaviour (e.g. Rest, 1994), one can be confident that clinic students will develop the necessary *sensitivity* to problems of ATJ. However, they still need the necessary *judgment* to know how best to respond and, given that empirical research repeatedly shows that ethical knowledge is only weakly connected to ethical behaviour (e.g. Rest, 1994, pp. 21–22), the *commitment* to care about doing the right thing and the *courage* to resist competing pressures and temptations. Fostering and guiding the development of these three components is far more challenging.

To guide judgment, students must obviously be exposed to arguments about lawyers' moral responsibilities in relation to ATJ and the various ways in which they can be met. These range from devoting one's career to helping those most in need, such as by working in legal aid practices, advice agencies or law reform organisations, to engaging in various forms of pro bono work (most obviously providing legal services, but also training or otherwise supporting others doing so) or substantially reducing fees to indigent clients ("low bono"), and finally to financially supporting those who work at the ATJ coalface.[3]

Persuading students of their obligations to enhance ATJ is unlikely to be easy. Those who regard neo-liberal ideology as a matter of common sense are likely to respond that individual lawyers are not responsible for imperfections in the legal services market, which in the long run is the most effective means of enhancing ATJ. More left-leaning students might insist that the state should guarantee ATJ and that engaging in or financially supporting pro bono work or other organisations providing free legal assistance allows it to escape its responsibilities. But even if students resist the siren calls of neo-liberalism or optimism at its imminent demise, their commitment to a career enhancing ATJ will be tested by factors which flow from or are exacerbated by the neo-liberal hold on education and legal practice such as the desire to repay debts and more generally to benefit from the monetary investment in their education, whereas their commitment to engage in pro bono work or financially support ATJ will be tested by the long hours of much legal work, and the time and financial pressures involved in trying to balance work and family life (Rhode, 2004, pp. 166–173; Sommerlad, 2007, p. 202).

Nevertheless, both theory and growing evidence from USLC student diaries suggest that clinical experience can prompt students to commit to enhancing ATJ once they qualify. Thus development psychologists, especially those influenced by the Aristotelian focus on character development (see Nicolson, 2008, pp. 156–159, 165), point to at least three sets of factors associated with the repeated immersion in morally charged life-experiences which may help develop and sustain such commitment. One is that the exposure to flesh and blood people facing ATJ obstacles may, as the following quotations illustrate, evoke empathy or sympathy,

> The client came to the clinic really as a last chance saloon after being through solicitors working pro-bono and also the CAB. When I found out that the client had already been through so much it hit me personally and I felt sad for the client knowing that she had been through so many different loops trying to seek justice problems.

> The more the client talked about his last few months at his job, and how much he'd enjoyed his work before that, the worse I felt for him. ... I found myself feeling really terrible for him ....

Such feelings of empathy and sympathy are crucial in contributing to the development of a sense of compassion and personal moral responsibility (e.g. Hoffman, 2001). But other emotions may also play a similar role.

> The thing that makes me angry in cases like these is the fact that companies like these must rely on people not seeking legal advice and instead just accepting that they signed a contract, and therefore have no remedy if they wanted a refund. ... In a hard economic climate, people seem more willing to walk over others to protect themselves, and I'm glad that the Law Clinic gives me a chance to stick up for people who may otherwise be trampled.

A second important influence on moral development is the example set by role models. Here, lawyers who support clinic activities were frequently mentioned. Thus one student commented that "[i]t is very heartening to see how many people are prepared to give up their time and resources to come in and do training events for students". This sentiment was echoed by another's comments on the lawyers who volunteer for the USLC's evening advice sessions:

> I have been heartened by the strength of their commitment to the project and to the pro bono cause in general. The practitioners are very busy individuals who are giving of their time at the end of what I'm sure is a long and often

> stressful day and this gives me a degree of comfort about the profession I am planning to enter.

Even clearer in evincing a commitment to ATJ after graduation were two students who were inspired by a practitioner teaching Ethics and Justice. Thus her work as a legal aid lawyer and founder of an environmental law centre showed Isla that she "can work in private practice and still achieve her ultimate aim of helping others", whereas Seamus declared that by "putting something back into the community" through pro bono assistance of his client she had acted as "a positive role model" and been "inspirational to me for my own career".

Finally, a third factor affecting moral development is the feelings of satisfaction or regret evoked by events. For example, informing a client that her employment case had been unsuccessful was for one student

> one of the hardest things I've done in the law clinic from an emotional standpoint. This was partly due to the fact that mistakes were made on this case and I had a strong feeling of having let the client down.

Conceivably this experience is likely to make her more inclined to go the extra mile for future clients. Far more frequently, students highlighted their satisfaction at helping clients, with some indicating that this has made them think differently about their future careers. Thus Isla's satisfaction at helping a client who had been turned down by eight law firms, prompted her to state:

> I didn't start my law degree to 'make a difference'. My goal was simply to earn enough money so I can afford some of life's luxuries and have no financial troubles. However, having seen the positive effect my time and effort has had on clients of the clinic has changed my perspective and now, my ultimate goal is to find a job that provides both financial security and a chance to help communities or less fortunate individuals.

In addition to these specific influences on moral development, students frequently cited their clinic experience more generally and the shared USLC ethos as influencing their attitudes to ATJ as the following show:

> When I started on the path to a law degree ... I thought I believed in access to justice for all; that judicial justice shouldn't just be the preserve of those with the money to pay for it. Having spent more time, and become involved in the work of the Law Clinic, I now know that I believe in access to justice, not just as a theory, but in practice.

> The most remarkable thing that has struck me is that my drive for access to justice has actually increased in my time in the clinic whereas I thought there was a risk that this spark would disappear once I got into the swing of things. This I believe is down to the attitude of the whole Clinic which keeps advisors motivated to strive towards assisting many people in the best way possible.

In some cases, appreciation of ATJ problems led to the assertion of an intention to play a role in redressing them once in practice, as these entries illustrate:

> Since losing his appeal, everywhere he has turned, the door has been closed. CAB refused to assist; firms of solicitors were also ignorant of the law, and also declined. Such ignorance deprives those most in need of access to justice, and a fair outcome. ... Surely it is essential that justice is accessible to all, regardless of who they are? That is the overriding reason why I want to work in the legal profession.
>
> Once I become a practising solicitor, I hope to continue pro bono work as helping people without expectation does make you feel good about yourself and increasing access to justice will provide more people with the legal expertise required to resolve their dispute.

Even more emphatically, Calum stated, "[b]efore my experience in the Clinic, I had imagined a career in a large law firm and hadn't really considered the larger ideal of social justice .... Now I find it impossible not to".

But these were not empty words. Calum now works for a law centre. More generally, many of those students whose diaries have been analysed and are now in practice have, like Isla, acted upon their stated intention to pursue a career which serves social justice or, like Seamus, fulfilled their stated commitment to engage in pro bono assistance, as well as donating to the USLC. Indeed, so many USLC alumni have returned to staff evening advice sessions that it has doubled the number of clients advised each year.

Access to justice and clinic models

However, while these anecdotal observations about the link between clinical experience and post-graduation behaviour are echoed by many others [see references cited in Nicolson (2008, p. 165, n. 124)], Sandefur and Selbin (2009) found that, when (recollected) attitudes students had when entering US law schools were controlled for, there was no evidence of clinical experience developing, as opposed to sustaining pre-existing commitments to engage in pro bono or practise law for the benefit of others [see also Rhode (2004, Ch. 7) and Granfield (2007) on more wide ranging pro bono programmes which also include externships and legal research projects, but cf. the more positive findings of Schmedemann (2009)]. Of course, sustaining student altruism is no mean achievement itself given the generally negative impact US legal education has on students' altruistic motivations for practising law (Granfield & Veliz 2009, pp. 53–54) and *homo œconomicus'* increasing presence in contemporary society. However, in addition to possible differences in pre-existing altruistic attitudes between US students and those entering the USLC,[4] and in the impact of their legal education on such attitudes (Nicolson, 2013, pp. 41–43), differences in clinic[5] orientation and resultant student experiences might also be important.

The in-house clinic model adopted in most law schools is one which, as Sandefur and Selbin's reference to 'clinical *training*' suggests (2009, passim), prioritises teaching legal skills, how law operates and sometime also legal ethics. Usually clinic involvement is limited to one or perhaps two semesters (though US students may take more than one clinical class), and the focus on student learning dictates low staff–student ratios and caseloads. In too quickly dismissing clinics as a beachhead for resisting the neo-liberal turn Thornton (2010, pp. 83–84) has in mind such 'educationally-oriented' (EO) clinics, which she correctly sees as too expensive to involve many students being exposed to issues of social justice.

By contrast, social-justice oriented (SJO) clinics, particularly if wholly or largely extra-curricular, have a number of advantages in this regard which suggest a greater impact than that of curricular EO clinics (Nicolson, 2006, 2015). Supervision and training need only ensure that clients gain acceptable levels of service rather than maximising student learning, thus allowing for much higher staff–student ratios and hence more students serving more clients. In addition, students can remain in extra-curricular clinics for the duration of their studies. While this will expand the breadth of their experiential learning, its quality can be enhanced by classes devoted to exploring the ethics and justice of law, legal practice and the legal system and providing students with opportunities for the sort of guided reflection which is essential to make the most of experiential learning in general (Brayne *et al.*, 1998) and community service in particular (Wizner & Aiken, 2004; Schmedemann, 2009; Adcock, 2013; Morin & Waysdorf, 2013). As an example of such a 'hybrid' clinic (Nicolson, 2006), for a budget of around £80,000 a year, the USLC has over 200 student volunteers – approximately a third of all law school students – who remain members for up to five years in which they represent up to two clients at a time, as well as assisting solicitors in evening advice sessions and engaging in other forms of community service such as public legal education programmes in schools and prisons, supporting gender violence survivors, law reform work and investigating miscarriages of justice.

Compared to EO clinics, SJO clinics thus have economies of scale which allow ATJ to be better served both directly by redressing more unmet legal need and indirectly by ensuring students a more extended exposure to the sort of clinical experience which may develop or at least sustain a commitment to enhancing ATJ on graduation. Arguably, they have other advantages in regard to this latter goal. One is that prioritising student education in law clinics implicitly conveys to students that their interests – now educational but later commercial – trump those of clients and the community. Moreover, choosing cases in terms of their educational value rather than client needs [as some clinics apparently do (Nicolson, 2006)] reduces the chances of learning lessons about the dire state of ATJ and the satisfaction to be gained in helping those affected.

Secondly, three features of extra-curricular clinics enhance their potential to successfully transmit their more altruistic message and to provide an alternative to neo-liberal modes of legal practice. One is that long-standing involvement in a distinct organisation, with perhaps a constitution, elections or an appointment process for committee positions, creates conditions conducive to a strong, cohesive ethos which can be transmitted through AGMs and committee meetings, as well as formal and informal social events, and other forms of informal socialisation which arise when people are involved in working close with and forming friendships with like-minded colleagues (cf. Jackson *et al.*, 1995). Secondly, because students often help run such clinics, they are more likely to feel a sense of 'psychological ownership' in 'their clinic' and its goals. According to empirical research, this tends to lead to them going the extra mile in fulfilling their responsibilities (Pierce *et al.*, 2001; O'Driscoll *et al.*, 2006), but it may also reveal to students a more effective and civilised alternative to the 'new managerialism' of legal practice, which has replaced collegiality with hierarchical discipline (Sommerlad, 1995). Thirdly, students who give up time to help run the clinic as well as helping clients involve altruistic role models.

However, notwithstanding the USLC's relatively cost-effective model, resource limitations and the commitment to select students who are primarily motivated by social justice mean that around half of the 120 or so students who apply each year are turned away. Consequently, their desire for experiential learning is met by arranging opportunities for externships in legal advice agencies and participation in the USLC's public legal education programmes. And, in order to maximise the potential for these experiences to raise awareness of ATJ problems and to inculcate a commitment to redress them, these students are also offered classes which, in addition to developing relevant legal and transferable skills, encourage them to reflect on their experiences in the light of reading and class discussion on ATJ and legal ethics.

Admittedly, such potential is already rather limited given that many of these students have already been judged to lack the necessary altruism for USLC membership and none will be subjected to the socialisation effects of a cohesive organisation with a strong social justice ethos, while those engaging in public legal education will not learn from the emotionally charged experience of helping those who would otherwise lack legal assistance. However, for law schools which cannot afford an EO or a curricular SJO clinic, or who do not have staff willing to support extra-curricular clinics, other forms of active learning will certainly go some way to accommodate students who are motivated to study law in order to serve justice. It will also enable the exploitation of less altruistic students' thirst for greater engagement with legal practice for the purposes of instilling an awareness of ATJ problems and a commitment to their redress.

The pejorative connotations of 'exploitation' might however raise ethical eyebrows. Utilitarians will respond that any harm to students is justified by the overriding benefit to the community. Certainly, it is arguable that any such exploitation is less than that involved in EO clinic students "practising on the poor" (Thornton, 2010, p. 83), rather than for the poor. But even in terms of Kantian ethics, students involved in clinical programmes which prioritise social justice are not treated *merely* as a means to such ends. Even if not formally trained to ensure a quality service to clients, they cannot but acquire enhanced employability, skills and knowledge from clinical work, as well as management, team-working and other valuable 'transferable skills' in helping to run clinics. Moreover, as long as law schools make clear that their clinics prioritise client and community needs over educational goals and that clinical classes include a focus on ethics and justice, prospective students are always free not to participate or to apply to universities with EO clinics.

Similar arguments suggest that the increasing desire by universities to enhance graduate employability is not being exploited when they fund clinical programmes which openly prioritise social justice. More fundamentally, however, it might be argued that universities should never prioritise community service over student education (see e.g. De Klerk, 2007, p. 98). In response, it can be noted that it has been recognised since at least Humbolt's nineteenth century vision of universities that they contribute to the common wealth through research as well as teaching. Today this extends to 'knowledge exchange/transfer' whereby universities share learning, ideas and experience with the community (Thornton, 2010, Ch. 5). Admittedly, many might see this more in terms of marketing the products of research rather than public service, but Thornton herself notes that neo-liberalism has encouraged stronger university links with the community (Thornton, 2010, p. 206). Indeed, the University of Strathclyde showcases the USLC as fulfilling its founding mission as a 'place of useful learning' notwithstanding its strong entrepreneurial focus (Clark, 1998).

But even as regards universities' educational mission, SJO clinical programmes arguably make no less a contribution than EO programmes. Thus, their goal of instilling in students a commitment to ATJ is more closely aligned to that of liberal legal education of producing good citizens. Moreover, while EO clinics seem to have the edge as regards developing vocational skills and knowledge, their more indirect acquisition by far more students in SJO clinics might well lead to greater overall educational enhancement.

More fundamentally, it can be asked whether those who pay for legal education are likely to object to clinics prioritising community service over education. Fee-paying students can always apply to universities with EO clinics, but may in fact prefer to opt for the longer-lasting and more varied practical experience of extra-curricular SJO clinics, especially if access to intensive clinical classes is rationed. And to the extent that legal education is publicly funded, it seems unlikely that many tax-payers will baulk at law schools seeking to redress the fact that many of their graduates currently do not repay the privilege of a publicly funded legal education by reducing unmet legal need.

Conclusion: towards an activist legal education

While this article was primarily directed at exploring the role of ATJ in legal education, less directly it sketches a more general vision of legal education which adds to the growing consensus that the distinction between the liberal and vocational approaches to legal education is artificial and overly rigid (e.g. Hepple, 1996; Johnstone, 1999; Boon & Webb, 2010). Instead, this vision – like that of Goldsmith (1999, 2002; Goldsmith & Bamford, 2010) – sees student involvement in work environments as an effective – if not the most effective – means of pursing the goals of a critical legal education through encouraging students to reflect on how law actually operates, its justice as well as access to justice and the ethical implications for practitioners. Such an education combines the focus on theory, context, justice and ethics which characterises a liberal legal education with the engagement with legal practice which characterises a vocational legal education in a way that is aimed at producing law graduates who see justice as part of their professional calling (Nicolson, 2013).

While as regards the teaching of law, ethics and justice, this approach can be better described as critical rather than liberal, the term 'activist' better captures its overall aims and methods. Thus, it seeks to foster activists for justice, whether social justice more generally especially as regards those who do not enter legal practice, or substantive legal justice and access to justice more specifically if they do, and pursues these goals through providing opportunities for active learning in the context of legal practice.

The theoretical focus on critique and context should appeal to those who share Thornton's vision of a socially liberal legal education. The practical focus should appeal to students and universities who demand greater vocationalism, and to high street and legal aid practitioners who want graduates with the sort of skills, knowledge and experience developed in law clinics and externships and to compete for the best graduates with the more powerful large law firms. The latter are likely to be ambivalent about an education which seeks to produce graduates who are more practice-ready, but less ready to practise for the benefit of those with the deepest pockets rather than those in most need or, as Luban (1988, p. 83) says, for "the person-in-no-trouble, but-who troubles-others" rather than the "person-in-trouble". And although Bradney (2003) wants to resist the profession's demands for graduates ready to make money for their employers, the unashamed espousal of a particular view of legal practice and particular set of values rather than another (altruism rather than materialism) in an activist legal education seems also to conflict with his idea of an education exposing students to competing views but not seeking to privilege some over others. But just as market control distorts economic markets, I would argue that the dominance of the large law firms in the recruitment market justifies seeking to ensure something like a level playing field as regards competing professional visions. Furthermore, while engaging more with legal practice *might*, as the opponents of vocationalism argue, be unfair to the many law graduates who do not enter legal practice (at least if one thinks that law schools can teach law sufficiently accurately, critically or ethically without engaging with practice), not doing so is unfair to those who do go into practice, if not also to the many more who hope to do so, and certainly to those who suffer from problems of access to justice.

At the same time, despite believing strongly that law schools should pursue an activist agenda, there is no reason why its content should replicate that outlined in this article. There are many other issues (human rights, gender, race and class, for example), which could become the focus of pervasive attention, many other forms of experiential learning (problem-based learning or simulated practice scenarios, for example) which can be used, and myriad ways law schools can combine these two activist dimensions depending on particular interests, pedagogical beliefs and political commitments. Nevertheless, the vision sketched in this article should appeal to those who are convinced that students and academics who directly benefit from legal education have a moral obligation to promote justice, while simultaneously responding to many of the directly opposed pressures which stem from the forces of neo-liberalism.

No doubt, there may also be ways to resist the rising tide of neo-liberalism in legal education and legal practice other than encouraging students to engage in activities which prioritise serving those most in need of ATJ. However, clinics and other forms of experiential learning are likely to appeal to both universities and legal employers in thrall to the vocationalism and profit maximisation goals of neo-liberalism in that they help ensure that law students become practice-ready. In this way, neo-liberalism itself creates a space which law schools can exploit to simultaneously make students 'justice-ready' (Aiken, 2012) in recognising their responsibility to act, not just as self-interested sellers of legal services to those who can afford their fees, but also as justice warriors intent on ensuring that legal services are available to all in need.

Acknowledgements

I would like to thank Hilary Sommerlad for initial suggestions as to content and reading, James Campbell for his superb research assistance, and an anonymous reviewer for helpful comments.

Disclosure statement

No potential conflict of interest was reported by the author.

Notes

[1] See Webb *et al.* (2013) and the special edition of *The Law Teacher* [2014, 48(1)] devoted to debating its implications.

[2] For a more detailed analysis of the diaries and the methodology used, see Nicolson (2010).

[3] Indeed, it is arguable that such financial contributions via a levy on practising certificates should be the default position for all lawyers unless they can establish some role in enhancing ATJ (Nicolson, 2012).

[4] Prospective members must persuade an interview panel that the student is more interested in furthering social justice than their own needs – though as Isla and Calum show, this process is not fool-proof.

[5] The following comparison is confined to in-house clinics given that the US pro bono programmes researched are so wide-ranging and not confined to serving those facing ATJ obstacles [less than 50% in Granfield (2007)].

References

Adcock, C. (2013) Beyond externships and clinics: integrating access to justice education into the curriculum, *Journal of Legal Education*, 62(4), pp. 566–575.

Aiken, J.H. (2012) The clinical mission of justice readiness, *Boston College Journal of Law & Social Justice*, 32(2), pp. 231–246.

Ashley, L. & Empson, L. (2013) Differentiation and discrimination: understanding social class and social exclusion in leading law firms, *Human Relations*, 66(2), pp. 219–244.

Baldwin, J. & McConville, M. (1977) *Negotiated Justice: Pressures to Plead Guilty* (London, Martin Robertson).

Bloch, F. (1982) The andragogical basis of clinical legal education, *Vanderbilt Law Review*, 35(2), pp. 321–354.

Boas, T.C. & Gans-Morse, J. (2009) Neoliberalism: from new liberal philosophy to anti-liberal slogan, *Studies in Comparative International Development*, 44(2), pp. 137–161.

Boon, A. (1998) History is past politics: a critique of the legal skills movement in England and Wales, *Journal of Law and Society*, 25(1), pp. 151–169.

Boon, A. & Webb, J. (2010) The legal profession as stakeholders in the academy in England and Wales, in: F. Cownie (Ed) *Stakeholders in the Law School* (Oxford, Hart Publishing), pp. 65–96.

Boon, A. & Whyte, A. (2010) Will there be blood? Students as stakeholder in the legal academy, in: F. Cownie (Ed) *Stakeholders in the Law School* (Oxford, Hart Publishing), pp. 185–224.

Bradney, A. (1995) Raising the drawbridge: defending university law schools, *Web Journal of Current Legal Issues 1*. Available at: http://www.bailii.org/uk/other/journals/WebJCLI/1995/issue1/bradney1.html, accessed 21 May 2015.

Bradney, A. (2003) *Conversations, Choices and Chances: The Liberal Law School in the Twenty-first Century* (Oxford, Hart Publishing).

Brayne, H., Duncan, N. & Grimes, R. (1998) *Clinical Legal Education: Active Learning in Your Law School* (London, Blackstone Press Ltd).

Brownsword, R. (1999) Law schools for lawyer, citizens, and people, in: F. Cownie (Ed) *The Law School: Global Issues, Local Questions* (Aldershot, Ashgate/Dartmouth), pp. 26–40.

Clark, B.R. (1998) *Creating Entrepreneurial Universities: Organizational Pathways of Transformation* (Oxford, IAU Press).

Clarke, J. (2004) Dissolving the public realm? The logics and limits of neo-liberalism, *Journal of Social Policy*, 33(1), pp. 27–48.

Davis, G., Cretney, S. & Collins, J. (1994) *Simple Quarrels: Negotiations and Adjudication in Divorce* (Oxford, Clarendon Press).

De Klerk, W. (2007) Unity in adversity: reflections on the clinical movement in South Africa, *International Journal of Clinical Legal Education*, 12, 95–104.

Francis, A. (2005) The business context: legal ethics, the marketplace and the fragmentation of legal professionalism, *International Journal of the Legal Profession*, 12(2), 173–200.

Genn, H. (1987) *Hard Bargaining: Out of Court Settlement in Personal Injury Actions* (Oxford, Clarendon Press).

Genn, H. (1999) *Paths to Justice: What People Think and Do about Going to Law* (Oxford, Hart Publishing).

Genn, H. & Paterson, A. (2001) *Paths to Justice Scotland: What People Think and Do about Going to Law In Scotland* (Oxford, Hart Publishing).

Goldsmith, A. (1999) Standing at the crossroads: law schools, universities, markets and the future of legal scholarship, in: F. Cownie (Ed) *The Law School: Global Issues, Local Questions* (Aldershot, Ashgate/Dartmouth), pp. 62–101.

Goldsmith, A. (2002) Why should law matter – toward a clinical model of legal education, *University of New South Wales Law Journal*, 25(1), pp. 721–747.

Goldsmith, A. & Bamford, D. (2010) The value of practice in legal education, in: F. Cownie (Ed) *Stakeholders in the Law School* (Oxford, Hart Publishing), pp. 157–184.

Granfield, R. (2007) Institutionalizing public service in law school: results on the impact of mandatory pro bono programs, *Buffalo Law Review*, 35(5), pp. 1355–1412.

Granfield, R. & Veliz, P. (2009) Good lawyering and lawyering for the good: lawyers' reflections on mandatory pro bono in law school, in: R. Granfield and L. Mather (Eds), *Private Lawyers & the Public Interest: The Evolving Role of Pro Bono in the Legal Profession* (Oxford, Oxford University Press), pp. 53–72.

Guth, J. & Ashford, C. (2014) The legal education and training review: regulating socio-legal and liberal legal education? *The Law Teacher*, 48(1), pp. 5–19.

Harris, P. & Beinart, S. (2004) A survey of law schools in the United Kingdom, 2004, *The Law Teacher*, 39(3), 299–366.

Harvey, D. (2005) *A Brief History of Neoliberalism* (Oxford, Oxford University Press).

Hazelkorn, E. (2008) Learning to live with league tables and ranking: the experience of institutional leaders, *Higher Education Policy*, 21, pp. 193–215.

Hepple, B. (1996) The renewal of the liberal law degree, *Cambridge Law Journal*, 55(3), pp. 470–487.

Hoffman, M.L. (2001) *Empathy and Moral Development: Implications for Caring and Justice* (Cambridge, Cambridge University Press)

Jackson, E.F., Bachmeier, M.D., Wood, J.R. & Craft, E.A. (1995) Volunteering and charitable giving: do religious and associational ties promote helping behaviour?, *Non-profit and Voluntary Sector Quarterly*, 24, pp. 59–78.

Johnstone, G. (1999) Liberal ideals and vocational aims in university legal education, *Web Journal of Current Legal Issues*, 3. Available at: http://www.bailii.org/uk/other/journals/WebJCLI/1999/issue3/johnstone3.html, accessed 1 April 2015.

Law Society and the General Council of the Bar. (1995) *Joint Statement on the Academic Stage of Training*. Available at: http://www.sra.org.uk/students/academic-stage-joint-statement-bsb-law-society.page, accessed 1 April 2015.

Law Society of Scotland. (2010) *Foundation Programme (Scottish Exempting Degree): Accreditation Guidelines for Applicants*. Available at: https://www.lawscot.org.uk/media/295010/foundation-programme-guidelines.pdf, accessed 1 April 2015.

Lee, R.G. (1992) From profession to business, the rise and rise of the city law firm, *Journal of Law and Society*, 19(1), pp. 31–48.

Luban, D. (1988) *Lawyers and Justice: An Ethical Study* (Princeton, N.J., Princeton University Press).

Luban, D. (2005) Lawyers as upholders of human dignity (when they aren't busy assaulting it), *University of Illinois Law Review*, pp. 815–845.

Luban, D. (2014) Is there a human right to a lawyer? *Legal Ethics*, 17(3), pp. 371–381.

McConville, M., Hodges, J., Bridges, L. & Pavlovic, A. (1994) *Standing Accused: The Organisation and Practices of Criminal Defence Lawyers in Britain* (Oxford, Clarendon Press).

Morin, L.A. & Waysdorf, S.L. (2013) Teaching the reflective approach within the service-learning model, *Journal of Legal Education*, 62(4), pp. 600–611.

Nicolson, D. (2006) Legal education or community service? The extra-curricular student law clinic, *Web Journal of Current Legal Issues*, 3. Available at: http://www.bailii.org/uk/other/journals/WebJCLI/2006/issue3/nicolson3.html, accessed 1 April 2015.

Nicolson, D. (2008) Education, education, education: legal, moral and clinical. *The Law Teacher*, 42(2), pp. 145–173.

Nicolson, D. (2010) Learning in justice: ethical education in an extra-curricular law clinic, in: M. Robertson, L. Corbin, K. Tranter, & F. Bartlett (Eds) *The Ethics Project in Legal Education* (London, Routledge), pp. 171–190.

Nicolson, D. (2012) Access to justice and the legal profession, *SCOLAG*, (416), pp. 133–136.

Nicolson, D. (2013) Calling, character and clinical legal education: a cradle to grave approach to inculcating a love for justice, *Legal Ethics*, 16(1), pp. 36–56.

Nicolson, D. (2015) "Our roots began in Africa": a multi-variate analysis of aligning university law clinics with social justice ends, *New York Law School Law Review* (forthcoming).

Nicolson, D. & Webb, J. (1999) *Professional Legal Ethics: Critical Interrogations* (Oxford, Oxford University Press).

O'Driscoll, M.P., Pierce, J.L. & Coghlan, A-M. (2006) The psychology of ownership: work environment structure, organizational commitment, and citizenship behaviours, *Group and Organization Management*, 31(3), pp. 388–416.

Partington, M. (1988) Academic lawyers and 'legal practice' in Britain: a preliminary appraisal, *Journal of Law and Society*, 15(4), pp. 374–391.

Paterson, A. (2011) *Lawyers and the Public Good: Democracy in Action* (Cambridge, Cambridge University Press).

Pierce, J.L., Kostovsky, T. & Dirks, K.T. (2001) Towards a theory of psychological ownership in organisations, *Academy of Management Review*, 26(2), pp. 298–310.

Rawls, J. (1999) *A Theory of Justice* (Cambridge, Mass, Harvard University Press, revised edn).

Read, J. (2009) A genealogy of homo-economicus: neoliberalism and the production of subjectivity, *Foucault Studies*, 6, pp. 25–36.

Rest, J.R. (1994) Background: theory and research, in: J. Rest & D. Narvaez (Eds) *Moral Development in the Professions: Psychology and Applied Ethics* (Hillsdale, NJ, Lawrence Erlbaum Associates), pp. 1–26.

Rhode, D.L. (2004) *Access to Justice* (Oxford, Oxford University Press).

Sandefur, S.R. & Selbin, L. (2009) The clinic effect, *Clinical Law Review*, 16(1), pp. 57–107.

Sarat, A. & Scheingold, S.A. (2001) *Cause Lawyering and The State in a Global Era* (New York, Oxford University Press).

Sauder, M. & Espeland, W.N. (2009) The discipline of rankings: tight coupling and organizational change, *American Sociological Review*, 74(1), pp. 63–82.

Schmedemann, D.A. (2009) Priming for pro Bono: the impact of the law school on pro Bono participation in practice, in: R. Granfield & L. Mather (Eds) *Private Lawyers & the Public Interest: The Evolving Role of Pro Bono in the Legal Profession* (Oxford, Oxford University Press), pp. 73–94.

Sommerlad, H. (1995) Managerialism and the legal profession: a new professional paradigm, *International Journal of the Legal Profession*, 2(2–3), pp. 159–185.

Sommerlad, H. (1999) The implementation of quality initiatives and the New Public Management in the legal aid sector in England and Wales: bureaucratisation, stratification and surveillance, *International Journal of the Legal Profession*, 6, pp. 311–343.

Sommerlad, H. (2007) Researching and theorizing the processes of professional identity formation, *Journal of Law and Society*, 34(2), pp. 190–217.

Sommerlad, H. (2008) Reflections on the reconfiguration of access to justice, *International Journal of the Legal Profession*, 15(3), pp. 179–193.

Thornton, M. (2010) *Privatising the Public University: The Case of Law* (London, Routledge).

Thornton, M. (2012) The new knowledge economy and the transformation of the law discipline, *International Journal of the Legal Profession*, 19(2–3), pp. 265–281.

Webb, J. (1999) Post-fordism and the reformation of liberal legal education, in: F. Cownie (Ed) *The law School: Global Issues, Local Questions* (Aldershot, Ashgate/Dartmouth), pp. 228–260.

Webb, J., Ching, J., Maharg, P. & Sherr, A. (2013) *Setting Standards: The Future of Legal Services Education and Training Regulation in England and Wales* (London, Legal Education and Training Review). Available at: http://www.letr.org.uk/wp-content/uploads/LETR-Report.pdf, accessed 1 April 2015.

Wizner, S. & Aiken, J. (2004) Teaching and doing: the role of law school clinics in enhancing access to justice, *Fordham Law Review*, 73, 997–1011.

The role of ADR in developing lawyers' practice: lessons from Australian legal education

KATHY DOUGLAS
Graduate School of Business and Law, RMIT University, Melbourne, Australia

ABSTRACT *Alternative dispute resolution (ADR) in legal education is an important area of study to ready law students for the rising use of ADR in justice systems around the world. In spite of the move towards ADR in legal practice, law schools internationally continue to debate the merits of including this area of study as a mandatory course in the legal curriculum. In Australia there have been increasing calls for the review of ADR in the legal curriculum and many lobby for the mandatory inclusion of ADR. However, if ADR is made a mandatory part of legal education in Australia it will be important that the way ADR is included ensures that students will experience the full benefits of studying this disciplinary area. The article outlines some of the benefits and challenges of including ADR in the legal curriculum. It draws on qualitative research with ADR teachers in law schools in Australia that analysed the most valuable approaches to including ADR in the legal curriculum. Analysis of the data gathered from twenty-nine ADR teachers shows the importance of skills based and experiential learning in ADR methods, the complexity of the issue of where to place the study of ADR, the difficulties of finding staff with sufficient expertise to teach in this area and the challenges of gaining support for typically costly teaching methods in the current environment of reducing funding for higher education.*

Introduction

Lawyers' engagement with alternative dispute resolution (ADR) is common in Australia due to the widespread use of mediation and other ADR options in court-connected contexts (Sourdin, 2012a). To varying degrees, ADR has also been adopted in court systems in the United Kingdom (Genn, 2010), Europe (Alexander, 2006; Steffek & Unberath, 2013), North America (Menkel-Meadow, 2012) and Canada (Macfarlane, 2008). Due to its increasing prevalence, legal scholars and professionals argue that this discipline area needs to be taught in law schools to ensure that students are prepared for the current demands of practice where the need to represent clients in ADR processes is becoming more commonplace (Macfarlane, 2008; Sourdin, 2012b; Duffy & Field, 2014). In Australia influential stakeholders, such as the Law Council of Australia (Corbin *et al.*, 2015, p. 512) and the Australian Council of Law Deans are recommending the inclusion of ADR in the list of mandated areas of study for admission to practice. A recent major report into Access to Justice by the Productivity Commission argues that legal education should be reviewed to ascertain the best ways that ADR can be introduced to law students (Productivity Commission, 2014). This report highlights the benefits of ADR in providing a speedy set of processes, ranging from mediation and conciliation to early neutral evaluation and arbitration, that may be more satisfying for parties than litigation.

In order to prepare lawyers for contemporary legal practice, law schools need to include ADR in some form in the legal curriculum (NADRAC, 2012; Duffy & Field, 2014; Productivity Commission, 2014). However, with the growing recognition of the imperative to include ADR, other questions arise as to the best ways to include this discipline area. Should ADR be included as a stand-alone course or in combination with the closely aligned discipline area of civil procedure? How important are the skills and role-play pedagogy common in ADR courses? Where should ADR sit in the legal curriculum and who should teach ADR? What is the likely cost challenges if experiential pedagogy through role-plays is widely adopted? This article draws from a doctoral thesis into the teaching of ADR in legal education in Australia. It provides some lessons learnt to answer these questions in the implementation of ADR into the legal curriculum. These lessons are relevant to all law schools internationally who are contemplating including ADR as a core part of the legal curriculum and to admission authorities who are considering making ADR a mandatory component of lawyers' education. The article discusses research that gathered primarily qualitative data through a series of interviews with ADR teachers undertaken in two states in Australia, Victoria and Queensland. The particular focus of the research was on the teaching of negotiation and mediation in ADR subjects, as these areas contribute most to the development of expertise in ADR in lawyers' legal practice.

The legal profession and dispute resolution

ADR is of course not a recent invention; throughout history dispute resolution processes have been used, in a wide variety of forms, in traditional communities around the world including Indigenous communities in Australia (Astor & Chinkin, 2002). Since the 1980s the Western approach to conflict has been increasingly influenced by the use of interest-based negotiation and mediation. This has led to significant interest in the use of ADR processes in court and to assist in settlement of litigation through collaborative problem solving (Sourdin, 2012a). ADR and particularly mediation can save on the costs of disputes due to the avoidance of a court hearing. Generally ADR provides parties with more control over the process (Astor & Chinkin, 2002; Boulle, 2011; Sourdin, 2012a; Productivity Commission, 2014). In mediation, party self-determination through agreement by consensus is a key part of the process (Boulle, 2011). The recent Productivity Commission report notes that "ADR can also be less formal and more culturally appropriate than a court or tribunal hearing and this may suit some parties" (Productivity Commission, 2014, p. 286). Familiarity with ADR can temper the traditional adversarial mindset of lawyers and develop non-adversarial practice where lawyers do not automatically resort to the courts. Instead lawyers consider a range of dispute resolution processes, fitting the dispute to the most appropriate option (Macfarlane, 2008). Such processes can also deal with non-legal issues such as relationship concerns and give parties the opportunity to deal with the full range of issues in a dispute (Boulle, 2011).

There are also significant criticisms regarding ADR in court-connected contexts. These relate to the decreased access of citizens to courts and the linked decrease in court funding (Genn *et al.*, 2013). In the early 1980s Abel (1982) argued that the use of private ordering, that is, decisions and solutions reached outside the public realm of the court, results in power shifting to the bureaucracy and away from the courts, with the potential likelihood that disadvantaged groups are discouraged from pursuing their legal entitlements. Similarly, Fiss (1984) warned of the dangers of a settlement culture in the law. He feared that imbalances in resources would prevent the poorer party in litigation from gathering and analysing sufficient information to assess the case against them and to make a judgement of fair settlement terms. Financial pressure may thus result in the acceptance of a relatively low amount, or encourage a race to an early settlement rather than a full exploration of options. Further, the high cost of litigation may force settlement even where a party has a meritorious claim. The experience of a trial tests evidence and assertions in a way that most private ordering processes cannot achieve. These concerns continue to be expressed as privatised justice becomes the norm and an over reliance on ADR arguably causes reduced access to the courts (Genn, 2010).

Even given these concerns there has been continued widespread growth in ADR and the use of mediation and other processes in court-connected contexts, and this has led to the need for a change in the professional identity of the legal profession. Lawyers' understanding of ADR affects the construction of their identity and influences the ways that they practice (Macfarlane, 2008). As noted by the influential Australian National Alternative Dispute Resolution Advisory Council (NADRAC):

> Lawyers increasingly play a role in advising clients about and guiding them through ADR processes. Regulatory provisions directly and indirectly require lawyers to advise clients on appropriate dispute resolution options other than litigation, including ADR. (NADRAC, 2012, p. 5)

Reviews of the Australian justice system have consistently pointed to the need to expand the use of ADR to improve access to justice and provide an alternative to the formal nature of litigation (e.g. Victorian Law Reform Commission, 2008; National Alternative Dispute Resolution Advisory Council, 2009; Productivity Commission, 2014). Legislative initiatives have attempted to shift the adversarial frame of much of Australian legal practice through obligations to engage in ADR as part of case management or as pre-litigation requirement (Sourdin, 2012a). Also, in Australia there is a duty for solicitors, under the *Australian Solicitors Conduct*

Rules, rule 7.2 to advise a client of any alternatives to litigation and these alternatives will commonly include negotiation and mediation. Despite these initiatives promoting ADR in legal practice, Australian processes such as mediation may focus on rights with little party engagement (Boulle, 2011; Sourdin, 2012a; Rundle, 2013). For example, in a study into lawyers' engagement with mediation in the Australian state of Tasmania, Rundle found that:

> Lawyers' use of court-connected mediation . . . inevitably reduces the attention that might otherwise be paid to individual non legal interests . . . Lawyers tend to have a narrow understanding of the purposes that can be pursued in court-connected mediation; focused primarily on settlement and the narrow legal definition of problems. (Rundle, 2013, p. 60)

Evidence of this kind shows that even given the wide use of mediation in court-connected contexts, some lawyers still fail to understand the differing advantages and disadvantages of ADR processes, particularly mediation.

Legal education and ADR

An appreciation of the benefits of ADR in the legal curriculum has been expressed in a number of reports. For example, in the United States of America a report into legal education, known as the Carnegie report, valued the teaching of ADR in legal education for the experiential learning gained by students through engaging with role-plays (Sullivan *et al.*, 2007). The report argued that such pedagogy assists students to build a professional identity that includes ADR. In the United Kingdom, a major report into the future of legal services and training (Webb *et al.*, 2013) ranks understanding of the discipline of ADR as of mid-range importance (see Webb *et al.*'s Table 2.4). Examples of the integrated inclusion of ADR can be found in the Missouri law school that includes "a required small section first year course Lawyering: Problem Solving and Dispute Resolution" (School of Law, University of Missouri, 2015).

As noted earlier in this article, in Australia various reports endorse the use of ADR and the need to study this area in our legal curriculum. Another example of this kind of endorsement relates to revised Australian educational standards in law that were published in 2010. These standards include ADR in a number of areas, most notably where students need to understand how to advise on dispute resolution options and demonstrate communication skills (Duffy & Field, 2014). The standards are not presently part of any accreditation requirements of law programmes, but have begun to influence the content and pedagogy of law subjects.

With the increasing interest in ADR in legal education, research was undertaken by NADRAC (2012) into the degree to which ADR is being taught in Australian law schools. The quantitative study was undertaken by NADRAC in 2010–11 and involved surveys being sent to all law schools. The data showed that eight out of twenty-seven law schools that responded to the survey included ADR as a mandatory course where at least 50% of the subject was devoted to ADR (NADRAC, 2012). Content relating to ADR was most often combined with civil procedure. In twenty-five law schools ADR was included in some form predominately as an elective. The report argued that more law schools should include this discipline area as a mandatory part of the legal curriculum because "the increased uptake of ADR means that it is important that law students, the future members of the legal profession, understand the major ADR processes" (NADRAC, 2012, p. 5). NADRAC final comments included the following statement:

> It is NADRAC's view that the amount of ADR teaching that currently occurs in the majority of Australian law schools is not sufficient in light of the increasing role that lawyers will play in advising clients about and assisting them in ADR processes. Clients, professional bodies and courts/tribunals expect that lawyers will be knowledgeable about ADR options and will also understand interest-based negotiation. (NADRAC, 2012, p. 12)

ADR in legal education has a great deal to offer law schools, law students and the legal profession. Sourdin (2012b) argues that it provides education that shapes law students' professional identity to include the full spectrum of dispute resolution processes, not merely litigation. Expertise in dispute resolution also allows law students to consider potential employment as mediators and dispute resolution managers, thus diversifying legal practice (Menkel-Meadow, 2012, p. 163). Crucially, ADR also offers students an experience of learning that focuses on experiential pedagogy through the use of role-plays in contrast to the commonly used content-driven lectures and seminars of many law courses (Duffy & Field, 2014). It is argued that ADR is best placed at the beginning of a law degree so that students are taught of alternatives to court and collaborative problem-solving skills before their understanding is moulded by litigation paradigms (Lande & Sternlight, 2010). There are a variety of ways to include ADR in the legal curriculum including as a stand-alone course, combined with another course discipline area (such as civil procedure) and integrated as modules in one or more courses in the programme (Moffitt, 2010). The inclusion of ADR with civil procedure, presently the most common approach to including ADR in the legal curriculum in Australia, can have advantages but may present a number of dangers for the teaching of ADR. Integrating ADR with civil procedure means that students experience the full range of dispute resolution options and do not see ADR as a separate and isolated option (Lande & Sternlight, 2010). However, litigation paradigms may be dominant in a combined course and leave little room for the content and pedagogy of ADR. The theory of ADR may be given scant attention with the pressure to teach two discipline areas in one course. The distinctive pedagogy of ADR, with its focus on role-plays, may be sacrificed due to higher costs of the provision of this kind of learning.

The benefits of learning about ADR and the impact on students of this kind of content and pedagogy have been demonstrated in two studies: in the United States of America and Australia. The first study was undertaken by Pipkin between 1990 and 1991 (1998). He compared the integration of ADR into first year law courses at the University of Missouri-Columbia with a control university at Indiana University-Bloomington where the first year curriculum did not include an integrated approach to the teaching of ADR. This study tested students' learning in respect of

ADR, where ADR was studied as a module in a substantive law course. Additionally, Pipkin investigated ADR teaching as a stand-alone subject at a third university, Willamette University. Students responded to questionnaires before undertaking the experience of the relevant subjects at the three law schools. The questionnaires used a series of statements to test orientations to legal practice with responses recorded on a Likert scale. Students were again surveyed after completion of the course using the same instrument, to test the effectiveness of their learning of non-adversarial orientations to practice, and the use of ADR. The responses to the surveys clearly showed the benefits to students of studying ADR, particularly in developing an understanding of ADR options and collaborative problem solving.

The second study was conducted in 2005 by Fisher *et al.* (2007) at La Trobe University, Victoria, Australia and was similar in nature. Again, through the use of questionnaires, researchers investigated whether the attitudes of law students regarding the use of ADR in legal practice shifted after experiencing a first year, semester-length stand-alone course dealing with ADR. In the research, students responded to a series of statements using a Likert scale that tested their attitude to litigation and ADR. Students were later re-tested to assess changes in their attitudes. The study showed that students experienced attitude changes to the ways that they framed legal practice. Students moved from a more adversarial approach to legal dispute resolution to one that privileged collaborative problem solving. This research clearly demonstrated the potential of the study of ADR to temper the adversarial mindset and provide students with skills in collaborative problem solving.

The research reported on in this article complements these research studies on student learning regarding ADR through a qualitative study that included in-depth interviews with ADR law teachers. This article discusses selected themes from the research. The data show important lessons that are relevant for any law school contemplating the adoption of ADR into the legal curriculum.

Research methodology

Qualitative data about the experience of teaching ADR was obtained through interviews with twenty-four teachers in Victoria and Queensland who taught ADR or a combination ADR course – that is where ADR was combined with another discipline area such as civil procedure. Data were gathered from a further five ADR teachers in Queensland through a survey. The survey instrument used a Likert scale and mirrored the questions posed in the interviews. The data were gathered during late 2007–08, with some surveys being returned in 2009. In the study there were thirteen courses and course guides analysed including ten ADR stand-alone courses and three courses where ADR and civil procedure were combined. Participants' responses were de-identified and coded. Coding used alphabetical letters of 'V' for Victoria, or 'Q' for Queensland to signify the state the law school was located, a number indicated the university and an additional alphabetical letter indicated if more than one person was interviewed or surveyed at the university. The page number of the transcript is also provided in any quotes.

Lesson 1: the importance of a skills focus in ADR to shape lawyers' professional identity

Analysis of the data gathered shows that all the participants in this study recognised the value of ADR as an alternative to litigation processes, and endorsed the teaching of ADR as contributing to lawyers' professional identity in a changing dispute resolution environment. All teachers, whether teaching stand-alone ADR courses or ADR courses combined with civil procedure, saw the need for lawyers of the future to understand and make choices amongst a range of dispute resolution options. For example, participants stated that:

> I think that it's critical that aspirant lawyers are exposed to a range of material about dispute resolution and processes and not be thrown into material which suggests that adversarialism is the only way to go. [V 2 (a) p. 3]
>
> . . . the role of lawyers is to assist people to resolve disputes and to do that well requires them to have this diagnostic function which has preventative aspects to it but also once you've got a problem then it's looking at that [dispute resolution] spectrum and really having litigation as only one minor option amongst many more dominant, non-adversarial options. [Q 2 (a) p. 1]
>
> I think [students are] given a useful framework for trying to understand what being a lawyer is about. I mean even basic things like having to do a negotiation, which the more 'adversarial' students thought, oh that will be easy-peasy, and then discover that it's really difficult, you know, that negotiation is a hard skill and one you can continuously improve. [V 5 (c) p. 3]

These quotes highlight the universal sentiment in the sample that ADR is an important part of law students' understanding of legal practice. Many of the participants also emphasised the need to counter adversarial constructs of practice through the study of ADR. Similarly, NADRAC in its report into ADR in legal education endorsed the role this subject area can have "... in contributing to a less adversarial culture in relation to dispute resolution" (NADRAC, 2012, p. 12). Additionally, a majority of participants described the central role of skills teaching in their curriculum. For example, participants commented:

> Yeah, and so that's really, should be the foundation I think of ADR practice for lawyers, is negotiation skills, then you build on that an understanding of other processes including mediation, arbitration as well, but then you need some . . . process skills for those various processes. [V 3 (a) p. 8]
>
> It's a skills-based subject, okay, so that our students come out with skills. And this is [about] skills, a communication skill, negotiation skills and rudimentary mediation skills. [V 2 (b) p. 13]

These teachers believed that the main vocational contribution of ADR centred on building negotiation and mediation skills in law students. The skill-building focus was emphasised in all courses that dealt with ADR as a stand-alone course.

Importantly, two of the three ADR courses that were combined with civil procedure lacked a skills focus, as these courses dealt with ADR through lecture/seminar material and omitted experiential learning. Only one of the three courses in ADR combined with civil procedure used a skills process and included collaborative problem solving. This is an important finding of the research as it exposes the risk that including ADR in combination with civil procedure in a law programme may not necessarily provide ADR experiential skills-based learning. Reassuringly, one of the three courses that combined ADR and civil procedure did include such learning. This course demonstrates that experiential learning can be included if such learning is valued by the law teacher and the law school. If ADR does become mandated in the Australian legal curriculum it will be important that law schools guard against the expedient inclusion of ADR in a civil procedure course without reworking the curriculum to include experiential skills-based learning.

As well as integration of skills into law students' future legal practice beyond graduation, mediation and negotiation skills can also be immediately useful in students' personal lives. ADR courses generally involve a focus on communication skills for lawyers and usually teach skills such as empathic listening, summarising and reframing (Boulle, 2011). Several participants, in both Victoria and Queensland, commented on the opportunity to teach communication skills in these courses that were useful in students' personal as well as professional lives. One participant noted the positive feedback to her strategy of linking the course to broader life skills:

> The thing that I think worked well, and I had a lot of students say to me afterwards, things like this was the first subject I did in law school that actually has some real use not just as a lawyer but in every day life. So those sorts of comments were really good and I guess that's what I wanted them to get out of it that it was kind of related to their legal practice but it was much bigger than that. [Q 1 (b) p. 6]

Other ADR teachers, in both Victoria and Queensland, noted that positive student feedback usually linked to the realisation that the skills could be used beyond the legal context:

> It's intensive practical skills, it's taught by an enthusiastic crew. People routinely say things like, "This is the best course I ever did at uni[versity]", or "This is so practical. It's not just for work, it's also for my life skills". You obviously get that kind of buzz. [V 1 (d) p. 4]
>
> People like it because it's skilled, because it's different, because they're building something, a personal skill that's going to stay with them, whether or not they're lawyers. [Q 1 (a) p. 9]

Students of ADR may use understanding of negotiation and mediation in other employment, making it an area of knowledge that is especially relevant for all law students. As one teacher noted, negotiation and mediation skills are relevant for practice as a lawyer but also for other jobs that students may undertake:

> One of the primary objectives I think is to skill students up in processes that they're likely to encounter when they practise. I think there's broader objectives in that I do think that teaching ADR skills [gives skills] more broadly in terms of negotiation, even if they never practise as a lawyer, and also assists them in terms of facilitating meetings and a whole host of other communication skills. So I suppose on the one hand, you're actually skilling people up to work in legal practice, on the other hand you're also skilling them up with more generic skills that are useful in other professions ... no matter where they go after law school, which I think is appropriate these days, given that not everybody proceeds into ... practice. [Q 1 (c) p. 1]

Where much of legal education fails to take account of the fact that only 50% of law students will engage in traditional legal practice (Thornton, 2012, p. 274) the benefit of ADR in legal education is that it provides learning that gives law students skills for a variety of kinds of employment. It is thus an important part of legal education for students whether they plan on practising law or entering other professions.

Lesson 2: placement of ADR in the legal curriculum

The data in this research show that each university in the study included ADR in their curriculum. There was little uniformity in the way that ADR was taught to students. At the time of the study, three universities in the study included ADR as a stand-alone compulsory academic course. Three universities included ADR in a combined ADR and civil procedure compulsory course. Three universities provided ADR as an elective, preceded by a module integrated with earlier compulsory substantive law course(s). Another three universities provided ADR as an elective only. Participants also referred to various areas of ADR, primarily negotiation and mediation, being taught as a module in other substantive law courses such as first year contract law.

Of the universities that included ADR as a stand-alone academic course, one law school positioned the course as a first year compulsory course and two had ADR as a later year compulsory course. Placement of ADR in the first year of a law degree may allow students to more effectively appreciate the adversarial paradigms of most other substantive law courses. The aim is to include ADR early in a law programme so that non-adversarial approaches are part of a law student's "standard philosophical map" (Riskin, 1982) in place of the philosophy that disputes are decided by third parties in court. In this study, this approach was adopted in only one law school where ADR was a stand-alone course. Two out of three law schools that combined ADR with civil procedure included this course as a compulsory later year course. One law school included its combination course as a first year compulsory offering and had done so after a major curriculum review. The course was deliberately included as a first year offering in order to introduce students to dispute resolution paradigms that included both ADR and litigation options. In the interviews, the majority of teachers were of the view that ADR should be included as a first year course, to combat the adversarial constructs of much of the rest of legal education. There was strong support for a first year positioning of ADR, but no clear agreement on the way that this positioning might be achieved.

Another approach to the positioning of ADR is to include it in the teaching of other substantive law courses. Grounding legal skills in real world contexts drawn from problem-solving scenarios in substantive law courses provides situated learning for various skills including those taught in ADR (Giddings, 2010). Such an approach might mean that negotiation skills are part of a problem posed in contract law. In this study, in the law schools where ADR was integrated into substantive law courses and then offered as an elective in later years, the teachers stated that ADR was usually included in first year subjects, such as contract or tort law. One teacher described integration of various legal skills in the following way:

> So if you're teaching commercial law you must teach interviewing also, and you must assess interviewing ... if you teach torts, you must teach negotiation ... there [are] twenty of those skills units that are mandatory in [our] LLB degree and substantive teachers have to learn how to teach the skills modules. [Q 4 (b) p. 2]

According to one teacher, an integrated approach gave students the chance to practise ADR skills in a range of courses and provided more opportunities for building skills:

> You can expose them to a range of practices. It's difficult to create the space in which they can actually engage in those different practices simply by reason of time ... The idea is that there'll be material contained in a range of courses rather than there being a compulsory ADR course. [Q 3 (a) p. 3]

However, it can be problematic to integrate ADR, with the complexity of mapping the various legal skills, and potential resistance from other law staff. Also, staff who have to teach the skills may be likely to reduce the ADR content due to the competing need to include doctrine in their substantive law course. As one teacher noted in regard to their integrated curriculum:

> I think it [ADR] gets lost. Every time there's a curriculum review it gets mapped. So 2003 was the last curriculum review with a whole lot of transition stuff in the first year and skills and 'what not' were developed and done ... but since then things have dropped off and units have added things or discarded things so we've just done another curriculum review and it's getting mapped again. [Q 2 (a) p. 4]

Some participants in this study supported integration whilst expressing doubts about the lack of ADR expertise among teachers who taught the subjects where ADR was integrated. In NADRAC's report into ADR in legal education it was found that one of the barriers to teaching ADR is the lack of academics with sufficient expertise (NADRAC, 2012, p. 13). In the evaluation of integration of ADR into substantive law courses, discussed earlier in this article, Pipkin (1998) identifies lack of commitment and expertise of non-ADR teachers as a problem in some universities. One teacher believed this lack of expertise posed a significant barrier to the success of an integrated approach to ADR:

> ... one of the things about integrating it or having it [as a] more substantial part of the law curriculum is [teachers'] worry that they don't have any skill base to draw on themselves. [V 2 (a) p. 24]

One teacher suggested training staff in ADR skills to address this dilemma. Another advocated recruiting practitioners who could draw on their ADR experience, however, he noted that practitioners usually lacked the academic credentials that universities value:

> ... I also know integration is doomed to fail because it requires so much [in terms of] resources. You'd have to sack half your staff and you'd have to hire practitioners who have become academics. So you'd have to change the nature of your hiring policy, which the universities won't do. So integration is a noble ideal which will only succeed in a few places. [Q 4 (b) p. 10]

Some teachers in this study stated that only a limited amount of time can be devoted to ADR in a substantive law course as this area would have to be 'fitted in' to an already full curriculum. It is unlikely that an integrated approach to the inclusion of ADR would include in-depth discussion of the variety of models of ADR as the time devoted to ADR is constrained by its placement in a substantive law course.

The last option is to provide ADR as an elective choice. Where ADR is an elective this means that only a small percentage of the students in a particular law school will have the opportunity to study this area as an academic course. Therefore, a student's experience might be limited to hearing of ADR in another subject such as an introductory law course. The findings in this research show that teachers of ADR stand-alone courses in this study consistently argued that ADR should be a compulsory course in some form. This objective is achieved where ADR is combined with civil procedure courses, as civil procedure is a compulsory knowledge area for admission to practice in Australia.

Similarly, where ADR is integrated as a module in another law course, ADR will be compulsory if that course is compulsory, such as contract or tort law. Although these approaches assure student engagement with ADR, the quality of the learning and teaching experience in terms of theory and practice of ADR may not be assured. In two of the three courses where ADR was combined with civil procedure, the ADR component was marginal to the discussion relating to litigation. In one course that combined ADR with civil procedure there was some inclusion of ADR theory and practice, but it was largely constrained by the time it took to cover both discipline areas. It would appear that combining ADR with civil procedure reduces the class time and opportunity for exploration of ADR. Similarly, an integrated approach to the inclusion of ADR will generally mean that only a limited amount of time will be devoted to the theory and practice of ADR. In contrast, a compulsory stand-alone ADR course, as adopted in three of the universities in this study, gives the best opportunity for students to explore ADR theory and practice in depth as a complete semester is devoted to the area. In a compulsory course in ADR there would be more opportunity to explore the full range of ADR models and practices. Positioned in the first year of a law programme such a course would provide students with sustained engagement with non-adversarial practice and combat the dominant adversarial frames of much of the rest of legal education. This approach might also be combined with a curriculum that integrates ADR in later compulsory courses to ensure students learn of ADR in 'situated' contexts.

Lesson 3: the price of skills-based learning

In Australia a law degree contributes to the overall corporatist strategy of a university, adding to both income and prestige. Universities and law schools in Australia have undergone a great deal of change in the last few decades and corporate concerns have risen in prominence (Thornton, 2012). In the context of legal education, corporatism relates to

> the set of statements and practices about legal education produced by law schools, law teachers and legal scholars that emphasise and prioritise the accountability of teachers and students, the efficiency of the teaching process and the marketability of the law school. (James, 2004, p. 588)

The influence of corporatism in legal education is profound in both content and pedagogy.

Efficiency has also become a major issue in law school education as a result of insufficient funding for undergraduate courses in this area. In the Australian university education system, students pay for a part of their degree through government charges. Australian law students pay the highest fees on the fee scale for their degree, while the Federal government contributes to law schools the "lowest amount that it contributes to any discipline" (Lewis & Yousef, 2007, p. 10). Thus many law schools struggle to fund high-cost pedagogy, such as simulations and legal clinics (Giddings, 2010).

A strong theme that has emerged in this research is the degree to which ADR teachers, who taught in stand-alone ADR subjects, were affected by funding concerns. This concern was not evident for two of the law teachers who taught in subjects where ADR and civil procedure were combined. These teachers did not include experiential learning in their learning and teaching design.

The development of skills in negotiation and mediation can be a time-consuming and costly exercise due to the common use of experiential role-plays and small-group learning (LeBaron & Alexander, 2009). The tension of balancing cost considerations with providing quality learning in the skills of negotiation and mediation was a frustration for many of the research participants. For example, a law teacher in Queensland noted the strain on teachers when attempting this kind of pedagogy and the fact that many will abandon the approach:

> Well if you run any classes, skills class, it's very labour intensive both in organising role-plays and then supervising them. So it's very exhausting and hard work, and expensive to get the right number of people there. So given that, what most people do is they don't do it. They go back to theory, because skills teaching [is] too exhausting. [Q 4 (b) p. 14]

Similarly, a participant in Victoria expressed frustration with cost concerns in providing weekend intensive assessment of students' legal skills by industry coaches. In order to meet budget constraints the course assessment was changed to allow tutors to assess the ADR skills in tutorials, which could be described as less beneficial for student learning.

Cost was a consistent theme for every interviewee teaching in undergraduate law ADR stand-alone courses: each of the teachers in this category commented upon cost concerns. Those teachers who taught ADR as an elective, capped student numbers to ensure quality learning and teaching outcomes. However, this approach was not possible in undergraduate compulsory ADR courses where numbers could be as high as three hundred students. In these courses, cost concerns impacted on pedagogy and reduced the degree of small-group learning desired by teachers. Notably, cost issues were not a concern in the core ADR courses in the two postgraduate law degrees that were part of this study. Experiential learning was unthreatened in the ADR stand-alone course and the combined ADR and civil procedure courses that were core courses in Juris Doctor (postgraduate law degrees) programmes. Teachers in these two courses reported that if numbers were high, multiple classes were offered to ensure high quality pedagogy, or alternatively additional staff members were employed to assist the teacher. The Juris Doctor programmes are largely funded independently of Commonwealth government funding in Australia and thus have more resources available for pedagogy (Sainsbury, 2008). This suggests that present Commonwealth government funding of undergraduate law courses may be insufficient to teach ADR as a core course that builds skills through experiential learning. Thornton has argued that Australian universities seem to perceive law programmes as providing prestige for a relatively low cost (Thornton, 2012). However, the perception of 'cheap prestige' is not sustainable where there is inadequate attention to teaching legal skills, and most learning and teaching is confined to large lectures. This approach to learning and teaching limits the opportunities of law schools to provide quality legal education and scholarship.

The adoption of ADR by governments and courts, and to some extent the legal profession, means that in most instances ADR could be said to enhance the marketability of law programmes. In this respect the strengths of ADR are also its weaknesses. Pedagogies that value small-group learning through role-plays and skill development (Druckman & Ebner, 2008), a common approach in ADR teaching (Duffy & Field, 2014), are often expensive to run as compared to substantive law subjects offered in large lectures (Keyes & Johnstone, 2004, p. 550). Thus despite the potential benefits of ADR, the subject generally falls foul of the efficiency imperative of university corporatism. One of the academics who participated in this study was specifically asked by her Head of School to reconfigure an ADR course to reduce costs: "[The] brief was to sort of replicate the skills that were taught but not at the cost" [Q 2 (a) p. 8].

The cost-cutting measures experienced by law teachers who participated in this study point to the reduction in the potential of law students to learn from ADR if small-group teaching and experiential learning are threatened. The building of student understanding of non-adversarial practice, and the development of student expertise in the theory and skills of negotiation and mediation, risks being undermined in many law schools due to the pressure of corporate needs in universities.

Conclusion

This article suggests that the widespread use of ADR in Australian court systems supports the inclusion of ADR in the legal curriculum. Law schools may consider its inclusion because ADR contributes to the legal professional identity where non-adversarial practice is privileged by courts and government policy. The majority of teachers in this research study saw their role as building students' skills in negotiation and mediation to prepare them for legal practice. Also, according to the teachers, skills in negotiation and mediation skills prepared students to address conflict in their personal lives, and also in professions other than law. This is valuable learning given many law students in Australia will not practise law.

If ADR becomes mandatory in legal education the question then arises as to its form and placement in the curriculum. This is a key question in the development of ADR in legal education. The participants of the study expressed support for ADR as a first year course so that the inclusion ADR could temper the traditional adversarial frame of much of legal education. However, it was not clear from participants whether ADR should be included as a stand-alone course, should be a module in another course or should be combined with a core area of study such as civil procedure. Where ADR is combined with civil procedure this study showed that there is a danger that the content and pedagogy of ADR, including experiential skills learning, can be marginalised. There were also some concerns expressed by participants in this study that without dedicated ADR teachers the ADR theory and practice may not be adequately taught. Where ADR was a module in another course there was the danger that it would be taught by teachers unskilled in ADR who may incrementally dilute the area in their course through lack of commitment and expertise. There would appear to be a need for further research that investigates and compares the provision of ADR in differing forms in legal education and thus provides data to inform curriculum choices.

Notably, whatever the way that this discipline area is included as a mandatory course in the legal curriculum, this study suggests that cost is a concern in providing experiential learning as part of the ADR. The study shows that ADR skills development is under threat in some law schools from increased budgetary constraints. ADR teachers who taught stand-alone undergraduate courses where student numbers were not capped, expressed frustration that the positive student responses to their teaching and learning strategies were undermined by the corporatist concerns and the need to deliver the programme with ever decreasing support. For example, the widely adopted pedagogy of experiential role-plays debriefed in small groups by students and requiring teacher feedback to achieve skills development is a costly approach to teaching in this area that often risks reduction due to budgetary constraints. Some teachers in this study directly expressed this risk and reported requests to reduce tutorials focused on experiential learning or re-develop courses so that the costs could be reduced.

ADR in legal education is an important issue for the legal profession in Australia and internationally. The study provides some valuable lessons learnt about the implementation of ADR in the legal curriculum. These are that ADR should be included in the legal curriculum as a mandatory first year course to develop law students' identities as non-adversarial practitioners. Importantly, if ADR is mandated in the legal curriculum its vocational benefits may be undermined if it is combined with civil procedure without a commitment to experiential skills learning. There is a need to secure staff who have the necessary expertise to teach in this area. Finally, there is also a need to protect the integrity of ADR courses through the provision of funds to support experiential learning. Without the appropriate support of staff and funding, the quality of ADR in legal education would be compromised and may not provide the educational benefits necessary to prepare lawyers for contemporary legal practice.

Disclosure statement

No potential conflict of interest was reported by the author.

References

Abel, R. (1982) The Contradictions of informal justice, in: R. Abel (Ed) *The Politics of Informal Justice, (Vol 1) The American Experience* (New York, Academic Press), pp. 267–320.

Alexander, N. (2006) Preface, in N. Alexander (Ed) *Global Trends in Mediation*, 2nd Edn. (New York, Kluwer Law International), pp. xxvii–xxviii.

Astor, H. & Chinkin, C. (2002) *Dispute Resolution in Australia*, 2nd Edn. (Sydney, Lexix Nexis Buttworths).

Boulle, L. (2011) *Principles Process Practice*, 3rd Edn. (Sydney, LexisNexis).

Corbin, L., Baron, P. & Gutman, J. (2015) ADR zealots, adjudicative romantics and everything in between: lawyers in mediation, *University of New South Wales Law Journal*, 38(2), pp. 492–512.

Druckman, D. & Ebner, N. (2008) Onstage or behind the scenes? Relative learning benefits of simulation role-play or design, *Simulation and Gaming*, 39(4), pp. 465–497.

Duffy, J. & Field, R. (2014) Why ADR must be a mandatory subject in the law degree: a cheat sheet for the willing and a primer for the non-believer, *Australasian Dispute Resolution Journal*, 25(1), pp. 9–19.

Fisher, T., Gutman, J., & Martens, E. (2007) Why teach ADR to law students? Part 2: An empirical survey, *Legal Education Review*, 17(1), pp. 67–101.

Fiss, O. (1984) Against settlement, *Yale Law Journal*, 93(6), pp. 1073–1090.

Genn, H. (2010) *Judging Civil Justice: The Hamlyn Lectures 2008* (Cambridge, Cambridge University Press) pp. 121–125.

Genn, H., Riahi, S., & Pleming, K. (2013). Regulation of dispute resolution in England and Wales: a sceptical analysis of government and judicial promotion of private mediation, in: F. Steffek & H. Unberath (Eds) *Regulating Dispute Resolution: ADR and Access to Justice at the Crossroads* (Oxford, Hart Publishing), p. 135.

Giddings, J. (2010) Why no clinic is an island: the merits and challenges of integrating clinical insights across the law curriculum, *Washington University Journal Of Law & Policy*, 34, pp. 261–289.

James, N. (2004) Power-knowledge in Australian legal education: corporatism's reign, *Sydney Law Review*, 26(4), pp. 587–612.

Keyes, M. & Johnstone, R. (2004) Changing legal education: rhetoric, reality, and prospects for the future, *Sydney Law Review*, 26(4), pp. 537–564.

Lande, J. & Sternlight, J. (2010) The potential contribution of ADR to an integrated curriculum: Preparing law students for real world lawyering (2010), *Ohio St Journal on Dispute Resolution*, 25, pp. 247–298.

LeBaron, M. & Alexander, N. (2009) Death of the role-play, in: C. Honeyman, J. Coben & G. De Palo (Eds) *Rethinking Negotiation Teaching: Innovations for Context and Culture* (Saint Paul, DRI Press), pp. 179–197.

Lewis, J. & Yousef, R. (2007) Law schools struggling to maintain quality, *Law Society Journal*, 45(3), pp. 10–11.

Macfarlane, J. (2008) *The New Lawyer: How Settlement is Transforming the Practice of Law* (Vancouver, University of British Columbia Press).

Menkel-Meadow, C. (2012) Too many lawyers? Or should lawyers be doing other things?, *International Journal of the Legal Profession*, 19(2), pp. 147–173.

Moffitt, M. (2010) Islands, vitamins, salt, germs: four visions of the future of ADR in law schools (and a data-driven snapshot of the field today), *Ohio State Journal on Dispute Resolution*, 25(1), pp. 25–36.

NADRAC (National Alternative Dispute Resolution Advisory Council). (2009) *ADR in the Civil Justice System—Issues Paper* (Canberra, Australian Government Attorney General's Department).

NADRAC (National Alternative Dispute Resolution Advisory Council). (2012) *Teaching Alternative Dispute Resolution in Australian Law Schools* (Canberra, Australian Government Attorney General's Department).

Pipkin, R. (1998) Teaching dispute resolution in the first year of law school; an evaluation of the program at the university of Missouri-Columbia, *Florida Law Review*, 50(4), pp. 609–666.

Productivity Commission of Australia Inquiry Report. (2014) *Access to Justice Arrangements* (Volume 1).

Riskin, L. L. (1982) Mediation and lawyers, *Ohio State Law Journal*, 4, pp. 29–60.

Rundle, O. (2013) Lawyers' perspectives on 'what is court connected mediation for?', *International Journal of the Legal Profession*, 20(1), pp. 33–65.

Sainsbury, M. (2008) Intensive teaching of graduate law subjects: McEducation or good preparation for the demands of legal practice, *Journal of the Australasian Law Teachers Association*, 1(1), pp. 247–254.

School of Law, University of Missouri. (2015) *About CSDR*. Available at: https://law.missouri.edu/csdr/about.html, accessed 26 July 2015.

Sourdin, T. (2012a) *Alternative Dispute Resolution*, 4th Edn. (Sydney, Thomson Reuters).

Sourdin, T. (2012b) Not teaching ADR in law schools? Implications for law students, clients and the ADR field, *Australasian Dispute Resolution Journal*, 23(3), pp. 148–150.

Steffek, F. & Unberath, H. (Eds) (2013) *Regulating Dispute Resolution: ADR and Access to Justice at the Crossroads* (Oxford, Hart Publishing).

Sullivan, W., Colby. A., Welch Wegner, J., Bond, L. & Shulman, L. (Eds) (2007) *Educating Lawyers: Preparation for the Profession of Law* (New Jersey, John Wiley and Sons).

Thornton, M. (2012) The new knowledge economy and the transformation of the law discipline, *International Journal of the Legal Profession*, 19(2), pp. 265–281.

VLRC (Victorian Law Reform Commission). (2008) *Civil Justice Review: Report* (Victoria, Victorian Law Reform Commission).

Webb, J., Maharg, P. & Sherr, A. (2013) *Setting Standards; The Future of Legal Services Education and Training Regulation in England and Wales.*

The LLB as a liberal degree? A re-assessment from an historical perspective

PATRICIA LEIGHTON
University of South Wales, Pontypridd and IPAG Business School, France

ABSTRACT *Despite the major recent expansion of law degrees in England and Wales and their accepted place as the 'academic stage' of a lawyer's education, important questions remain or are even intensifying over their nature and content. It is said that there is an increasing urgency to develop broader and more liberal degrees, not least to respond to changes in the delivery of legal services and expertise but also societal imperatives. This article argues, through an exploration of historical data, especially from the nineteenth century, that the system of legal education that was developed and embedded during that period inevitably makes liberalising law degrees both problematic and challenging.*

Introduction

This article accepts that one of the major yet unresolved debates regarding legal education in England and Wales is the role and nature of the law degree, in particular, the extent to which it is or should be a liberal degree. This, in turn, is dependent on debates around the nature of legal education itself and raises basic questions of who is the education for, what and who determines its content and the interplay of the various stakeholders. These include the legal academics themselves who have been often curiously absent or ignored in these discourses but who over the years have been responsible for the wide and varied range of learning materials that this article argues are so important for understanding the culture of contemporary legal education.

The analysis reflects briefly on the origins and development of legal education, but focusses on what is argued to be the most critical period—that of the nineteenth century.[1] This period saw major legal changes but also the formalising of legal education, the flowering of law publishing, and also the rise of university teaching of English law. As well as considering the contributions of major academic and other commentators, the article draws on a range of both primary and secondary relevant source materials, including various reviews and surveys of legal education, the views of contemporary commentators and the records of legal education providers. However, particular reliance is placed on a hitherto neglected rich source. This is basic legal education materials. Included here is evidence of the law curriculum, the nature content and statistical data on examinations, learning materials, especially student books, and journals. There is also some consideration of student support facilities, such as libraries, journals and, importantly, coverage of the then law teachers and their work. In effect, the article relies heavily on evidence from the 'grass roots' and practical realities of legal education.

This article, therefore, in reflecting on the tensions within legal education explores these nineteenth-century sources and suggests that the structures, pedagogy and student learning materials that evolved in this period provide an explanation or part explanation of those tensions. It is argued that they are vital for a full understanding of the culture of legal education today, but also have direct implications for many of our currents debates, especially regarding the law degree.

Background

In setting the scene, a few points need to be made. The first is the relatively recent development of law degrees as major courses in higher education. For reasons that are not immediately clear, up to the 1960s courses were relatively few and by no means all universities offered them. Legal professionals, including judges, if they were graduates, tended not to hold a degree in law, favouring ones in classics and humanities. However, between 1964 and 1971 the number of law undergraduates doubled, largely through the rise of polytechnics, the expansion of the London University LLB and then the CNAA (The Council for National Academic Awards), a state-run degree-awarding body.[2]

Even so, in 1971 there were only an estimated 604 law teachers in England and Wales,[3] but by 1995 there were almost 2,000[4] and following dramatic expansion in recent years, especially of post-graduate provision in law, the numbers are likely to be far higher. Law degrees are to be found today in virtually all universities, even those such as Aston, Salford and York, traditionally unenthusiastic about law, but also in many newer and smaller institutions as well as the now important private sector providers.[5] However, despite this massive expansion, we also know that, beyond pedagogic change, the nature and content of law degrees has remained relatively unchanged for many years.

A second introductory point has to be that there is an intrinsic tension within law degrees, reflecting a wider tension in legal education generally, as to whether degrees are essentially the first stage of a vocational education or whether they are, or should be, freestanding opportunities to explore a wide range of issues not necessarily geared to the legal system or professional legal practice. These include ethics and values but also contextual issues, and perhaps historical and philosophical matters. Of course, this question raises the issue of the control and regulation of legal education but also whether the dichotomy between vocationalism and liberalism are really mutually exclusive or whether they can be effectively combined within a pluralistic system. Both of these questions are, of course, relevant for this article but beyond its scope.

There have been important official enquiries, starting with the 1846 Select Committee on Legal Education[6] (that, *inter alia*, called for law to be taught in universities), the *Ormrod Report*, 1972[7] (that created the three stages—academic, vocational and continuing—of current professional legal education), the Advisory Committee on Legal Education(ACLEC) Report 1996[8] (calling for an integrated programme of legal education with a liberal degree at its heart), along with many commentators exploring the 'vocational versus liberal' debate. Twining characterised the choice as between "Pericles and the plumber",[9] and Bradney, as education in ivory towers or satanic mills.[10] And, of course, famously, Dicey asked in 1883 whether law can be taught at universities at all?[11]

The aim of this article is not to add further comments on this long-running debate but to ask why legal education generally and law degrees in particular have such a distinct culture and, more importantly, why they seem so resistant to 'liberalisation'. This is not to criticise those who oppose change but to emphasise how strong the historical and cultural traditions of legal education are. It is argued that they are embedded not so much in where and by whom law is taught, but in the 'building blocks' of legal education—the key texts, pedagogy and assessment methods that have created such a powerful culture. In explaining this culture and resistance to change, many point fingers at the legal professions and before them the courts, that have controlled entry to the legal profession and have played a major role in determining the nature and content of law degrees. However, it is suggested that even if the role of professional bodies were weakened, and universities and law schools could themselves determine the nature of a law degree, it is likely little would change, so powerful are these embedded cultural factors.

It is, of course, also necessary to highlight the nature of the common law itself, especially its empiricism and pragmatism, as playing a key role in this culture. Sugarman, amongst others, has argued that the influence of the common law on the culture of legal education was intensified during a formative period at the end of the nineteenth century.[12] This was largely due to the influence of scholars from the USA, especially Langdell at Harvard, who argued that law was a science, was principled and coherent and best explained through the case law/Socratic Method as an effective inductive learning method.[13] Sugarman comments that "policy and politics were eschewed in the name of science" and that this, coupled with "the legal profession enjoying a monopoly over legal education" and therefore "loathe to permit university and professional jurists to challenge that monopoly", provided a strong bulwark against a liberal education.[14]

The origins of legal education

We have a richness of literature, harnessed by the Selden Society in particular, that has traced the origins of both the English legal system and legal education. This shows that the education system was managed exclusively by the profession, mainly in the Inns of Court and Chancery,[15] with the universities not teaching English law until the nineteenth century. This is, of course, in marked contrast to the position of law teaching and universities in the civil law jurisdictions. The education in England was severely practical, with mooting, case-putting and other exercises forming the backbone, coupled with Readings by eminent lawyers.[16] These included Coke and More in the sixteenth century but in reality, as judged by the content of the Pension Books of the Inns, the influence of the Readings has been exaggerated. Often they failed to take place, despite high fees paid to the Readers. If they did they were generally poorly attended and were likely of more symbolic value than educational value. Importantly, the Inns had very limited libraries and the benchers of the Inns seem to have had little interest in legal education. The few texts on law, such as Bracton,[17] were simply declaratory of the law and its rules and procedures. In truth, legal education until the nineteenth century was overwhelmingly 'learning by doing'. For the barrister it was pupillage; for the attorney and solicitor, articles.

So, coming into the late eighteenth century and the nineteenth century we have a picture of only two universities in England, neither of which taught English law, and of a profession which had limited educational facilities and activities, backed up by a tradition of apprenticeships for barristers, attorneys and solicitors, which appears to have been generally poorly supervised.[18] Nonetheless, the profession—in effect the judiciary, populated only by barristers—controlled entry to practice and had a monopoly on the criteria for entry. Of course, we did have Blackstone's *Commentaries* on the Laws of England, from 1769, followed by a number of Commentaries by other writers, and, though practical, they occasionally raised broader issues.[19] The *Commentaries* were designed to form the basis of legal education in universities. This, of course, did not happen.

These features of the origins of legal education led one eminent writer, Milsom, to conclude that "Lawyers have always worked with their eyes down",[20] untroubled by contextual, comparative or conceptual matters.

Change

The legal profession in England and Wales has been, in reality, a combination of different groups, typically subject to considerable mutual hostility. The Bar has always been London-based and tightly organised, self-contained and confident, not least as they exclusively gained access to the powerful judiciary. Attorneys in the common law courts and solicitors in the courts of equity were of low status and spread throughout the country but also had their own, albeit limited, organisations—the Inns of Chancery. Some buildings remain with us today—Staple Inn on Holborn, facing what was Furnivals Inn, though they were wound up in the nineteenth century. They, too, had Readings, often on procedural matters, and practical exercises, but again activity was often sporadic and more symbolic than real. Their Pension books and accounts show little interest in legal education, though the Chancery Inns did support libraries and were often used as venues for student meetings.[21]

In the run up to the political and legal reforms of the nineteenth century there was some nascent interest in legal education and the need for change. Interestingly, it was the attorneys that began to organise, form associations and, importantly, note the move towards written examinations for various professional roles, not least for apothecaries, the civil service and also for Oxford and Cambridge degrees. This seemed an interesting development to explore. The London Law Society, founded in 1825, aimed to dominate the profession, had built the prestigious building that exists today in Chancery Lane and began to exert influence on the judiciary, still charged with controlling entry to the Rolls. Things happened quickly. In 1833 a lecture series began. In 1836 written examinations were introduced for attorneys and in 1837 for solicitors. This was a defining moment for legal education.[22]

There are two aspects of this development of particular interest. First, judging by comments in and letters to the legal press at the time, the primary motivation for introducing the exams was not educational but to give the profession increased credibility. It was hoped that the exams would weed out the 'sharpers' and other undesirables that allegedly proliferated in the profession. A few pointed out that the sharpers were often rather bright and might do well in the exams! The second matter of interest is that the exams were not conducted by the judiciary but were, in effect, delegated to the Law Society, took place in its Hall and were quickly then referred to as the 'Law Society Examinations'. At the time the Law Society had in membership fewer than 10% of those on the Roll from London and the South East, so the actions of the leaders of the Society were both ambitious and opportunistic.

Given that these were vocational examinations the topics selected are unsurprising. They were Common and Statute Law, Conveyancing, Equity, Bankruptcy and Criminal Law. These were the self-same subjects that constituted the content of the Law Society's lecture programme from 1833. As the century progressed other subjects were added such as Ecclesiastical and Admiralty Law and, for example, Criminal Law was sometimes optional. An Intermediate Examination was added in 1861 that covered Contracts, Real Property, Equity and Book-keeping, with Stephen's *Commentaries* on the Laws of England being, in effect, the prescribed text.[23] A non-law Preliminary Examination was added also in 1861, and included History, English, Arithmetic, Latin, Greek and modern languages. Aside from the Preliminary Examination, there were no non-law subjects in the Examinations. In 1880 an Honours examination was added and graded students into, First, Second and Third Class Honours. Interestingly, even then there was a reluctance to award a First. Interestingly also, the Honours award was very prestigious with a high failure rate. Those holding the LLB appear to have been subject to a higher failure rate than those who had done the Intermediate examination. Some commentators found that amusing and a sad reflection of the poor standard of university examinations.

By the mid-1860s, the examinations were well established, and written examinations for the Bar were added in 1872. Such developments spawned a new and vibrant education 'industry', based on lectures, texts, student journals, summer schools, even correspondence courses ('monthly letters') and, most importantly, the professional law crammer. Passing these examinations was no easy matter with a steady failure rate of 40%. So, professional help was essential. Much as in recent years, there have always been concerns about 'too many lawyers' and 'too many' law students. The high and consistent failure rate was deliberately designed to address these concerns and pride was taken in the high failure rate. Perhaps this is one example of a contrast with today, where concerns have focussed on alleged 'grade inflation'?

What were the examinations like? Fortunately, as the Examinations were published until 1870 we are able to know quite a lot about them.

Taking the examinations in Conveyancing, initially the questions were very basic. The 1836 examination simply asked questions such as "What is an estate tail?", "At what age is a person capable of making a will?" and "For how long may an agreement for a tenancy be made by parole?". However, even by the second examination in Michaelmas 1836 the questions became slightly more complex. For example, it asked: "How is the personal property of intestates distributed?" and "How do judgments affect real property?".

Each examination paper contained 15 questions. Although questions tended to be simply knowledge-based, the incidence of repetition of specific questions was quite low, indicating the need to have wide knowledge. By the 1860s, some 'problem solving' question had emerged. An example would be;

> A and B are seisesd in fee of three estates which number 1, 2, and 3. They hold estate 1 as tenants in common, estate 2 as joint tenants and estate 3 as copartieniers. Can A and B or either of them by will devise their undivided shares in these three estates, or any, and if any, which of them?

We do not know from the examiners what answers they were expecting, at what length and in what detail. However, what we do know is that the crammers who prepared students for these exams (of which much more is said later) published model answers in their various journals. *Law Notes*, published by Gibson and Weldon, the leading crammers, is an especially useful source.[24] It can be seen that the suggested answers are clear and concise but appear not to require precise source references, though the model answers generally suggested the students refer to specific texts.

The Intermediate Examination, which was first sat in 1862, covered some of what we would call Foundation Subjects, including Contracts and Stephen's *Commentaries on the Laws of England*, referred to above, which might be referred to as a legal system course. For Contract, the questions were much as those for Conveyancing in the Final Examination. For example, "Give a definition of a simple contract" and "Give some instances of consideration sufficient to support contracts". However, the questions on Stephen's *Commentaries* could be more discursive. For example, the Lent Examination paper 1881 asked "What is the fundamental difference between fundamental law and natural law?". It is likely that the same pattern of stereotypical responses would be expected but one could ask whether the format of the assessments, especially their requiring a breadth of knowledge, albeit in a context of high failure rates, was so different from the situation today. Of course, many schools today do use innovative and highly demanding assessment formats. However, it is thought that the reduced role for both non-law and broader topics, the stagnant or declining role for course work, the rise of the MCT and an increasing tendency in some law schools towards short questions, each attracting, say, 5% or 10% of half the marks on a paper arguably indicate less change than one might expect. This is especially so in a context where assessment itself has been such an important topic for research and analysis, along with critical comment.[25]

One point needs to be made on the evolution of the examinations. At no point, from the judiciary, Law Society members, or writers to the many law journals in this period, did anyone call for a broadening of the assessment topics. All appeared happy with the practical and instrumental nature of the examinations.

How and where did law students learn?

Nineteenth-century law students, unsurprisingly, focussed on the examinations which quickly became rather predictable. When examinations were introduced in 1836/7 candidates must have been in shock as there were very few law texts, no earlier examination papers and no teachers, and so they muddled through initially. There were no universities teaching for this examination and, significantly, although this period coincided with the setting up of University and Kings College, London, they appeared to play no direct role. This means that given the fact of the need to pass examinations in order to practise, the years following 1936 are probably the defining period for the evolution of legal education.

As referred to above, the Law Society had, since 1833, run lectures at its premises. They attracted large numbers each year to courses that covered the subjects of the examinations. Each course had 12 lectures, generally delivered by barristers but they were expensive and one questions whether they were sufficiently focussed on the examinations to be really useful for clerks.[26] A comparison between the lecture contents and the examination questions indicates that the courses were more in the nature of updating/CPD for practitioners, as they dealt with topical issues rather than the basic topics of the examinations. For example, in 1843 the Conveyancing lectures covered new statutes on Wills, and on Limitations and the Law of Mortgages; the Common Law lectures dealt with "the law applicable to railways and Joint Stock Companies".

If the lectures at the Law Society were not sufficiently attractive to articled clerks, what of other learning sources? What of, for example, the university law schools, both in London and other parts of England and Wales?[27] They were surely preparing students for assessments on the basic principles of English Law? The London University LLB had attracted external students and gradually the so-called civic universities developed their own degrees. Contemporary commentators were not enthralled by university law schools. At Oxford from 1750 to 1850 there had been no lectures at all on civil law and at Cambridge it was reported that at Downing College in 1800, "the law school was recognised as refuge for those who were averse to intellectual effort".[28] Even in London, where University and Kings Colleges had taught law from their inception, although initially they attracted a wide range of students, attendance soon fell away.

Interestingly, in the latter half of the nineteenth century and especially outside London there were efforts to combine 'university law teaching' with training for articled clerks sitting the Law Society examinations. The civic universities in the north of England and the University of Wales set up Boards of Legal Studies that combined representatives from the professional bodies with the university law schools. This was an innovative and unique attempt to combine legal education for both university degrees and professional education.[29] Where numbers were not great this seemed a way to maximise efforts, reduce costs and support legal education on a partnership model.

The trail was blazed by the Manchester Law Association that initially set up well-attended lecture courses from 1844 on legal topics, most of which were useful for those entering the Law Society Examinations. The Manchester efforts metamorphosed into a Board of Legal Studies that worked with the Victoria University. The Liverpool Board of Legal Studies set up in 1886 had representatives from the university but also from the Liverpool Law Society and the Liverpool Law Students Association. Again, after an initial flurry of interest and some very experienced lecturers delivering a coherent set of lectures, the numbers had declined even by 1890.This pattern was replicated in other university centres whereby courses struggled to survive, especially if they were more 'academic' or 'liberal' in nature and therefore seen as irrelevant for the dominant formal structures of legal education—the Law Society Finals and the Bar Finals. There were, of course, some exceptions to this rather depressing picture. The Yorkshire Board proved very successful in attracting a range of students, as did the Board for Wales where summer schools attracted significant numbers. However, the Boards did not survive long.

The picture is further depressed by the fact that the Legal Education Association, founded in 1869 with wide support from practitioners and with a remit to create an inclusive and comprehensive system of legal education, also failed.[30] Many argue that it was the opposition of the Bar that was mainly to blame. Interestingly, the prime reason was probably that proposals tended to put universities in the 'driving seat', which, of course, caused alarm at the Inns and the Law Society. As noted earlier, the Select Committee on Legal Education, 1846, had called some 20 years earlier for a growing role for universities in legal education, but again to no avail. One can only conclude that some very powerful interests were able to prevent a national scheme of integrated legal education emerging that had, to an extent, proved effective at a local level. It might be relevant that London had not developed a Board of Legal Studies on the models successfully developed by Yorkshire, Manchester, Liverpool and Wales.

It is tempting to see this as an outcome of 'turf wars' whereby the Bar wanted to retain pre-eminence and the Law Society wished to consolidate its role in vocational legal education outside the Bar and Inns. However, in reality, the universities had not clearly established a role in legal education. Whatever the reason and despite the highly regarded publications by their staff/jurists the universities had a very limited role in teaching students. They had not made a case, or gained sufficient support for a free standing liberal education in law and were, in effect, very much the junior partners in any collaborative efforts. This position is in marked contrast to the situation in many continental states where, for example, the universities in Germany played such a dominant role. Indeed, looking at the national and legal professional press in England and Wales at the time, the universities are noticeable for their absence from most agendas and debates.

The rise of the crammers

If it was proving difficult to sustain lecture programmes both within and beyond the universities, where was it that most students prepared for their examinations? The answer was the so-called 'crammers'. Their history and role merits far more attention.[31] They were numerous, worked together in firms or on their own, used sophisticated marketing techniques such as advertising widely in law publications, publishing their claimed 'success rates', wrote numerous, well thought through student learning materials and achieved fame through writing texts. Some of these texts are well worth reading, not least for their 'student centred approach'. This was in marked contrast to the rather dull practitioner texts which students had had to use until the crammers emerged. Crammers taught in small groups, often in the evening and sometimes at weekends, and provided a generally cost-effective way for a student to pass their exams. As time went on, students tended to prepare with the crammers on a short, intensive, typically three-month basis, a pattern that intensified in the twentieth century.

Some crammers were mysterious and used initials or titles rather than their full names, such as Alpha, Lex, Examiner, R.H. and B.C., which may reflect the ban on advertising by lawyers. The following advert in the *Law Times* in 1855 is typical:

> Law Examination—Gentlemen prepared for their examination by an Attorney who has been eminently successful. Terms 15 guineas in advance; balance on passing. Address 'B.C.', Mr Hales, Law Stationers, 49a Lincolns Inn Fields.

With the introduction of the Intermediate and Preliminary Examinations for solicitors and especially the prestigious Honours Examination there was considerable growth in numbers of crammers but also market consolidation. Three firms dominated the last decades of the century. They were Gibson and Weldon that became the College of Law, Indemaur and Thwaites and Preliminary Law. Gibson and Weldon, for example, stated in the *Law Times* for 3 May 1890 that, "Of the 6 prizemen (In the Honours Examination) the first five were pupils of Messrs Gibson and Weldon; seven other pupils were in the first class … ". The leading crammers also dominated the law publishing market, a matter considered in more detail below, but also clearly had a well-developed and effective business model. The crammers were largely based in London, though Penningtons in Manchester, situated close to the university, achieved success in the early years of the twentieth century.

The examinations, as has been referred to earlier, became predictable to an extent. At the risk of stating the obvious, the examinations largely determined what was taught. The formats remained steady up to the mid-twentieth century. However, the potential range of questions was wide, requiring a thorough grasp of a whole legal subject. It is inevitable that the crammers became experts in both spotting questions and learning what 'worked' to pass. Their personal advice was often backed up learning support such as Gibson's *Law Notes* for students that survived until fairly recently. There is also evidence of active law student societies and publications, such as the *Legal Telegraph*, something we continue to encourage today and often see as part of the law school culture.

However, there were sometimes openly voiced concerns by the crammers themselves, as well as others, about the teaching methods used. In 1905, Gibsons proudly announced that their system of student preparation " ... is as far as possible that of a Law School and all ideas of preparing students on a 'cram' system is disregarded".[32]

One other general point should be made about the crammers. With the exception of Gibsons, crammers did not confine themselves to the Law Society examinations. They also prepared students for the Bar, law degrees, public and professional examinations, sometimes providing residential facilities, libraries, reading rooms etc. The crammers were, for the main part, teachers who were often working full-time and who were generally former practitioners. They focussed on the specific needs of examinations, were clearly effective in developing sound learning and communication skills (and might have met our current demands for employability!) but who operated within a narrow vision of what legal education is about. They did not play a part in formal curricular and assessment developments, so cannot be blamed for that narrow vision. They were just simple service providers who saw market advantages in responding to the format of the examinations and the high failure rate.

What is their legacy and why is it important?

This article has posed the question as to whether there ever has been a liberal law degree but more importantly, to enquire why attempts from 1846 to develop a coherent and cogent broader degree failed. It is now argued that although the 'iron cage' of the profession has been critical, coupled with weaknesses in the universities, there were other factors at work, especially deriving from the nineteenth-century crammers.

It is argued that the culture of our current legal education is far more dependent on these crammers than the traditions derived from leading jurists, academics or even the influence of other common law developments. These wider contributions are often seen as 'extras', evidenced by the hostility towards the inclusion of so-called 'non-law' subjects and their decline in recent years. Vital for this analysis is the nature, content and style of the learning materials students rely on. In particular, it is important to assess the text books and to note the very strong historic links of crammers with law publishing. Many crammers operated out of publishing firms' premises. Just as today, the law publishing market was highly competitive but also repetitive with texts on core subjects often looking very similar. Texts do not just explain legal principles they also give out messages through their style, packaging and general presentation to students about the nature of the subject they are studying. Even today texts are dominated by images of law courts, the legal profession, litigation or problem solving rather than law-making, law's social and other contexts, law enforcement and generally the effectiveness of law. And why would a nineteenth-century law student study economics, philosophy or business issues if they were not on any curriculum or examination paper?

Law texts

The history of law texts is a short one. There were, of course, early texts by Glanvil, Bracton and Coke's *Institutes*[33] that remained in print for, sometimes, centuries. There were, of course, many specialised texts dealing with specific topics, such as Littleton's *Tenures*, and case-books.[34] There were also practitioners' Pocket Books that dealt with procedural matters. An example is Jacob's *Attorney's Practise*,[35] still in print in 1825. Important was Blackstone's *Commentaries*, which the crammers published student guides to. Those guides were then themselves subject to other student guides. This prompted a correspondence to journals in that books were becoming repetitious and derivative, something that might resonate with us today?

Following the introduction of written examinations in 1836/7 the student would have had a number of practitioner texts that were applauded for their accuracy and clarity. They were often very detailed, long and dense. However, comprehensiveness and detail were seen as virtues—as they are for many today. However, the authors initially made few attempts to abstract the legal principles or, more importantly, made no attempts to explain the origins or rationale for the rules. There were exceptions. For example, Chitty's *General Practice*[36] was subject to comment in 1835 that "by examining the principles upon which rules are founded, thereby impressing the memory more deeply with their nature and effect".[37]

It might be noted that despite the general failure of the books to explore those general principles, the major works remained in print for decades and there appears to have been no demand for a different style of text. This is despite the major political, industrial and societal upheavals during even the early decades of the century. Of course, as the century wore on, texts on legal history, constitutional matters and many texts dealing with the rule of law, jurisprudence did emerge and were influential.[38] However, they did not impact on the student body more generally, which was to study for professional examinations or law degrees closely aligned to those examinations.

If the question of a liberal law degree is in part based on exploring both the content of the curriculum and the approach to legal topics, combined with appropriate assessment methods, there were a few student texts that met the second element (and very few at first). One such was Smith's 1846 *Law of Contract*,[39] a Law Society lecturer who tragically died very young. It is interesting to read his explanation for the highly debated doctrine of consideration in Contract law. He claimed that it was: "to guard persons against the effects of improvidence in entering hastily and inconsiderately into engagements which may prove ruinous to them". We might share that explanation but it does indicate that some texts were making an effort to provide a rationale for legal rules. Even today, we might read some books on the law of contract and note, not only the lack of any contract theory but of even basic explanations of 'why' some rules are there, or why they are neglected etc. An example might be the 'postal rules' and the very limited role for duress and undue influence to avoid apparent contractual liabilities.

Another perhaps enduring feature of these early student texts was that they appear very 'insular'—that is, they draw little on other writers of student texts.

Josiah Smith's 1855 *Compendium of the Law of Real Property and Conveyancing*[40] is an exception and he compares and contrasts the comments of other text book writers and the book emerges as far more lively and challenging than most.

Our popular case-books today have their origins not so much in the original law reports but in students' case-books written by those crammers. It has to be remembered that law reports until fairly recently were not always reliable or well set out. In 1837, and to an extent, 'out of the blue' came J. W. Smiths' *Leading Cases.*[41] It covered 61 cases, though it was rather ponderous in style. Cases are set out, followed by discussion and, interestingly, there is then a consideration of how the decision relates to other cases. It stands up to scrutiny today and, unsurprisingly, was followed by case-books on other subjects. Most reviewers of these texts were complimentary but some had reservations. For example, a writer to the *Law Magazine* wrote in 1845 that "he could think nothing more appalling than the sight of a new text book" most of which were to "profit or puff" the author.[42] He even gave a negative critique of Blackstone! It might also be noted that texts written by Law Society lecturers rarely survived long compared to the crammer texts, though no doubt one reason was that the crammers linked their teaching with those texts—much as many law teachers do today!

As well as standard texts, the student could access various guides, model answers and the principles upon which these books proceeded would be seen as educationally sound today. Some writers did try to break this rather convergent mode and, perhaps predictably, ran into a chorus of criticism. One such is John Shirley, whose *Leading Cases on the Common Law*, was first published in 1880.[43] It covers 150 cases and its importance lies in the way it handled the generally tortuous description of pleadings. As an example, the case of *Vaux v. Newman*, better known as the Six Carpenter case is set out.

> It was a warm September afternoon in the early days of James 1st that six thirsty carpenters entered a London tavern and there did buy a quart of wine and there paid for the same. Mark that, gentle reader, they paid for it. But a quart of wine does not go far with lusty working men; the reader will be scarcely surprised to hear that like Oliver Twist they asked for more . . . and our friends stoutly refused to pay.

Then follows a discussion of trespass ab initio and even the law of distress to which it was loosely connected. There then follows a clear statement of law and even ideas for the policy of the law.

Strong feelings were aroused by the text—some considering it "frivolous" but other reflecting on whether this was a good way to help students remember the cases. They then worried that the student would swallow the sugar but not the pill![44]

An assessment

The development and role of the crammers was but one element of legal education in the nineteenth and early twentieth century. Clearly, university legal education was emerging, sometimes in conjunction with the local legal profession. Some impressive legal academics were not only teaching but producing enduring critiques of English Law and contributing to debates on the future of legal education. However, overall, law degrees remained limited in their ability to attract students with the numbers using crammers far exceeding those attending university. This paper has posed the question of why the attempts to liberalise the law degree and to detach it from the profession/vocational programmes has failed to date. Many note and comment on this failure; some look at the role of regulation and professional body control. Few have looked closely at the hidden legal educators who so powerfully set the scene for the determining culture of legal education. Crammers are so often characterised as routine, of limited intellect, money-makers and caused a dumbing down of legal education from which we have never recovered. This assessment might need some review.

However, two points need be made. First, crammers were not the originators of the system they served. Indeed, many crammers lamented the narrowness and lack of enquiry but they were never part of the discussions and policy-making on legal education. Second, if examined in detail, their work and their texts reveal the application of sound pedagogic principles and a sense of supporting students in effective ways. In truth, they knew their business. And while the profession, the universities and leading writers have been failing to establish a blue print for recent and contemporary legal education, their methods, their culture and their influence has endured.

Acknowledgements

I should like to express my thanks to two people, in particular. The first is Graeme Broadbent from Kingston University who has made many insightful comments on earlier drafts of this article and with whom I have had many very helpful discussions. The second is David Sugarman from Lancaster University who gave generously of his time and expertise and provided much help on source materials. I should also like to express my thanks to other members of the Legal Education Research Network (LERN) with whom I have discussed this and other related areas of my work on the history of legal education.

Disclosure statement

No potential conflict of interest was reported by the author.

Notes

[1] Much of the primary data and other source materials relied on in this article are taken from an unpublished M. Phil. thesis on "The Education of Solicitors, 1825–1914" for Kings College, and the Institute of Education, University of London.

[2] *Ormrod Report* (1971) Cmnd 4595.

[3] *Ibid.* See also the records of the National Council for Academic Awards (CNAA) for 1965–1993. It made over 1.3 million awards involving 140 institutions, though it is unclear regarding the numbers of law graduates. Data can be accessed at the Modern Records Centre, University of Warwick. For more recent data on law degree student numbers and information about law courses and law schools more generally, see the three surveys of law schools, conducted by Professor Phil Harris between

1991 and 2004. See P. Harris & S. Beinart, A survey of law schools in the United Kingdom, 2004 (2005) 39 *The Law Teacher* 299. A useful source for basic statistical data is the Higher Education Statistics Agency (HESA). This indicates that after many years of sustained growth in undergraduate numbers, the last year (2013–14) has seen a decline of around 5% in full-time law undergraduate numbers from 2009–10 (11,325 to 10,110), which has prompted some of the debate on the future of the law degree. It should be noted that the HESA data do not include the private providers of law degrees.

[4] P. Leighton, T. Mortimer & N. Whatley, *Today's Law Teachers: Lawyers or Academics?* (London, Cavendish Publishing, 1995). To identify the main features and trends in law school provision, the three 'Harris' surveys are worth consideration, along with the earlier Wilson and Marsh surveys. See J. Wilson, A first survey of legal education in the united kingdom (1966) *Journal of the Society of Public Teachers of Law* 9; J. Wilson & S. Marsh, A second survey of legal education (1975) *Journal of the Society of Public Teachers of Law* 18; J. Wilson, A third survey of legal education in the United Kingdom (1993) *Legal Studies* 13; P. Harris, S. Bellerby, P. Leighton & J. Hodgson, *A Survey of Law Teaching* (London, Sweet and Maxwell and the Association of Law Teachers, 1993); P. Harris & M. Jones, A survey of law schools in the United Kingdom (1997) *The Law Teacher* 31; see Harris & Beinart, *op. cit.* for the 2004 survey.

[5] In mind here is the setting up and expansion so as to provide national coverage by providers such as BPP University Law School, founded in 1992 with six campuses and the University of Law, with seven, whose origins go back to 1876. There are also a considerable number of smaller, both public and private providers who offer law degrees validated by universities, including London University. The London University External Degree dates from 1858 and currently students are taught in 130 affiliated colleges world-wide. Around 2,000 students achieve the LLB each year .It remains difficult to accurately estimate total student numbers studying for the LLB. It might be noted that although some of the major private providers initially only offered preparation for the Bar and the Law Society, they now generally offer the full range of law programmes, including Masters degrees. Some of the private providers highlight that they are explicitly preparing law undergraduates for a career in the legal profession.

[6] *The Report of the Select Committee on Legal Education* (1846) Parliamentary Papers X.

[7] For an interesting critique of Ormrod, see, T. Mungham, English legal education: a commentary on the Ormrod Report (1972) 7 *Valparaiso University Law Review* 87. He notes the limited contributions made by law teachers, observing what appeared to be "their complete sense of inferiority".

[8] For a contemporary commentary see R. Grimes, The ACLEC Report—meeting legal educational needs in the 21st century (1996) *Legal Education Review* 12; P. Leighton, Comments on the ACLEC Report (1996) 30 *The Law Teacher* 201. Another useful source published contemporaneously with the ACLEC Report is O. Kahn-Freund, Reflections on legal education (1996) 29 *Modern Law Review* 121. Another excellent source is R. Hepple, The renewal of the liberal law degree (1996) 55(3) *Cambridge Law Journal* 470.

[9] Perhaps the most enduring and at the time, radical, contribution to the debate is W. Twining, Pericles and the plumber (1967) 82 *Law Quarterly Review* 83. In discussing law's suitability as an academic subject, he referred to critics of legal education stating it to be "narrow-minded, a remote form of life, chauvinistic, educationally unsophisticated and intellectually sterile" (at p. 92).

[10] Anthony Bradney has spearheaded the debates on the liberal law degree, arguing strongly for law as a topic of liberal study. For example, Anthony Bradney, *The Liberal Law School in the Twenty-first Century* (Oxford, Hart Publishing, 2003). See also Anthony Bradney, Aristocratic values, the liberal law school and the modern lawyer (2011) *The Web Journal of Current Legal Issues*. One might refer to the debates around H. Hart, *The Concept of Law* (Oxford, Oxford University Press, 1961), especially the contribution by A. Simpson, *Reflections on the Concept of Law* (Oxford, Oxford University Press, 2011), themselves considered by D. Sugarman, Brian Simpson's approach to legal scholarship and the significance of the reflections on the concept of law (2012) 3 *Transnational Legal Theory* 112. See also A. Simpson, Rise and fall of the legal treatise: legal principles and the forms of legal literature (1981) 48 *University of Chicago Law Review* 632. One might also refer to the debates and policy developments that have followed the ILEX Professional

Services, Bar Standards Board and the Solicitors Regulation Authority Report, *Setting Standards: The Future of Legal Services Education and Training Regulation in England and Wales* (2013). Although the main focus of the research and the report is professional training for the legal profession, it is inevitable that the role, nature and content of the law degree be seen as of great significance.

[11] A. V. Dicey, *Can English Law be Taught at the Universities?* (London, Macmillan, 1883).

[12] D. Sugarman, Making a respected gentleman out of law professionals: a commentary on Albert Venn Dicey *Can English Law be Taught at the Universities?* (2011) *Kultur und Beruf in Europa* 16.

[13] See Sugarman's powerful critique of this period in D. Sugarman, Legal theory, the common law mind and the making of the textbook tradition, in: W. Twining (Ed.) *Legal Theory and the Common Law* (Oxford, Blackwell, 1986).

[14] As a testimony to the intellect and influence of the jurists, it might be noted that some of their texts have survived to today, albeit with different authors! Anson's *Law of Contract*, first published in 1879, is today in its 29th edition; Pollock on *Torts*, first published in 1887, was in its 15th edition in 1951 and Clerk and Lindsell's *Torts* is today in its 21st edition. It is important to note that many of the authors of these prestigious texts themselves recognised the need to make them more accessible for students. For example, J. Salmond, *A Summary of the Law of Torts* (1912). Sometimes others wrote 'cut down' versions. For example, J. Mannooch, *An Analysis of Sir Frederick Pollock's Law of Torts for Students* (1911). for further consideration of the contribution of the jurists, see, R. Cosgrove, *Scholars of the Law: English Jurisprudence from Blackstone to Hart* (New York, New York University Press, 1996); N. Duxbury, *Frederick Pollock and the English Juristic Tradition* (Oxford, Oxford University Press, 2004); N. Lacey, *A Life of HLA Hart: The Nightmare and the Noble Dream* (Oxford, Oxford University Press, 2004). For a recent critique, see S. Bartie, The lingering core of legal scholarship (2010) 30(2) *Legal Studies* 345. Another interesting critique is from B. Tamana, *Failing Law Schools* (Chicago, Chicago University Press, 2012).

[15] There is a rich literature on the Inns of Court and those of Chancery. Of particular interest is J. Baker, *The Third University of England: The Inns of Court and the Common Law Tradition* (London, Seldon Society, 1990). The Inns of Chancery have received less attention, but see D. Bland, *A Bibliography of the Inns of Court and Chancery* (London, Seldon Society, 1965). The Chancery Inns were smaller Inns populated mainly by attorneys and solicitors and each Inn was associated with an Inn of Court. See W. Douthwaite, *Staple Inn* (1887); F. Day, *Staple Inn* (1887) and J. Ringrose, *The Inns of Chancery* (1909).

[16] J. Baker, *Readings and Moots at the Inns of Court* (London, Selden Society, 1990); D. Sugarman, A special relationship: American influences on English legal education 1870–1965 (2013) 18 *International Journal of the Legal Profession* 161.

[17] Bracton *Notebook* (A collection of cases from the thirteenth century), edited and translated by S. Thorne (Cambridge, MA and London, Harvard University Press and Selden Society, 1968–).

[18] For a nineteenth-century account of life as an apprentice see *The Diary of Thomas Loughborough*, 1832–4, Law Society Collection.

[19] Blackstone, *Commentaries on the Laws of England*, 2001 edn edited by W. Morrison (London, Cavendish Publishing, 2001).

[20] S. Milsom, *Historical Foundations of the Common Law* (London, Butterworths, 1969) at p. xii, Introduction. The whole of the Introduction is well worth reading as an overview not only of the evolution of law itself but of institutional matters and responses to it.

[21] See, for example, *Records of Barnard's Inn. 1621–1867* (Grays Inn Collection, 1960); *Pension Book of Clement's Inn* (Selden Society).

[22] The Law Society probably emerged from the Society of Gentlemen Practisers in the Courts of Law and Equity which had been founded in 1739 and was based in London. The Law Society had a small membership (only 224 in 1827 and by 1832 only 838). Although its membership grew to around 1,600 by 1858, it should be noted that only 327 were drawn from outside London. The various Law Societies or Associations in the major cities had higher membership and operated in a different way from the (London) Law Society. They were more closely integrated with professional and governmental bodies and were therefore strongly community based. Indeed, displeasure with the Law

Society led in 1847 to the setting up of the Metropolitan and Provincial Law Association (MPLA). It was wound up in 1895 following calls for one voice to represent the profession. Membership of the Law Society then grew considerably. For an excellent account of these developments and the role the profession was playing in legal developments more generally, see D. Sugarman, Bourgeois collectivism, professional power and the boundaries of the state: the private and public life of the law society, 1825–1914 (1996) 3 *International Journal of the Legal Profession* 81. Another way of considering the overall shape and representation of the solicitors' profession is to explore the role of the local law societies and associations. Membership was voluntary and it is clear from correspondence to the legal press that many outside London saw the Law Society as elite, remote and too London-centric. For example, of the 237 solicitors in Manchester in 1865 only seven had joined the Law Society; as late as 1895 only two out of 93 Leeds solicitors were members. There were, of course, many smaller towns where the Law Society had no members and perhaps the local solicitors belonged to no professional association. This position was in marked contrast to the Bar, where membership of an Inn was compulsory.

[23] S. Stephen, *Commentaries on the Law of England* (London, Butterworths, 1868).

[24] A. Gibson & A. Weldon, *Law Notes*, (London).

[25] See, for example, the newspaper article: Good degree awards not always in line with intake, *Times Higher Education* (17 April 2014) at p. 6.

[26] See generally, Volumes 11 and 12 (1835–6) *Legal Observer.*

[27] D. Winstanley, *Early Victorian Cambridge* (1940), at p. 3. The 1846 Select Committee on Legal Education was very scathing about the contribution of universities at the time. For a more recent account, see P. Maharg, *Transforming Legal Education* (Aldershot, Ashgate, 2007).

[28] One correspondent to the *Law Times (Vol.112, 1901–2)* at p. 486, stated: "You could pass the London LLB examinations on work you did for the Intermediate Law Society Examination". This may not have been accurate, but it was a frequently expressed view.

[29] For further information in the activities of these organisations, see the annual reports of, say, the Liverpool Board of Legal Studies, and the Wales Board of Legal Studies.

[30] See, for example, the Report of the Examination Committee on these developments in the Law Society's *Annual Report* for 1899. By this date all efforts to develop legislation to provide an integrated system of legal education had failed.

[31] One of the few sources is R. Kersley, *Gibsons 1876–1962; A Chapter in Legal Education* (1973).

[32] Marketing information by the firm; see Kersley, *op. cit.*, p. 113.

[33] 1628–1644.

[34] A. Thomas, *Littleton's Tenures* (1577, Rychard Tottyt).

[35] Jacob's *Attorney's Practise* (Nutt and Gosling, 1837). For an earlier example of this type of publication, see Bohun, *Practising Attorney or Layer's Office* (Crockat and Worrall, 1728).

[36] J. Chitty, *General Practice* (1837 edition).

[37] Comments to Vol. 10 (1835) *Legal Observer* 4.

[38] Many were on legal history, for example, F. Pollock & F. Maitland, *A History of English Law* (1898); F. Pollock, *English Law before the Conquest* (1899); and H. Maine, *Ancient Law* (1861).

[39] J. Smith, *Law of Contracts* (Stevens and Norton, 1846).

[40] J. (Josiah) Smith, *Compendium of the Law* (Stevens and Norton).

[41] J. Smith, *Leading Cases* (Stevens and Norton).

[42] *Law Magazine* 1829 onwards. The publisher up to 1856 was W. Benning and from the Butterworths. The quote is from the June 12, 1845.

[43] J. Shirley, *Leading Cases.*

[44] See a correspondent to *Law Notes* vol. 10 (1891), p. 320.

Legal education without the law – lay clients as teachers and assessors in communication skills

Wilson Chow & Michael Ng
Faculty of Law, The University of Hong Kong, Hong Kong, China

Abstract *This paper reports an empirical study of the use of simulated clients to assess (facilitate the learning of) interviewing skills and communicative competence of law students at the University of Hong Kong (HKU) from February 2013 to April 2014. In this period, about 400 HKU Postgraduate Certificate in Laws students participated in interviewing exercises with simulated clients, who are lay persons trained to portray clients in a realistic manner and to assess communicative competence by standardized rubrics designed in Scotland since 2006. HKU Faculty of Law is the first law school in Asia to adopt this standardized client program to assess law students' interviewing skills. The paper will present the data analysis of assessment results of the students and their evaluation of this experiential learning program. Our analysis confirms the reliability and validity of using standardized clients as assessors of interviewing skills. It also reveals the necessity of modification of the original design of standardized client program, particularly in relation to the assessment aspect of it, according to specific cultural and commercial needs in an Asian business city like Hong Kong.*

I. Introduction

A framework of essential and transferable skills is necessary for competent professional practice. The ability to communicate effectively in daily legal practice with lay people is one of those skills. A group of teachers, who are also alumni, of the Postgraduate Certificate in Laws ('PCLL', similar to the Legal Practice Course in England and Wales) at the University of Hong Kong ('HKU'), reflecting on their learning experience in the PCLL at different times and their early days of legal practice, strived to provide the next generation of lawyers with a more direct and realistic learning of oral communication skills. As a result of such passion, belief and continuous effort in searching for a solution, the use of simulated clients ('SCs') to teach and assess the interviewing skill and communication competence of law students began in Hong Kong at HKU PCLL in 2012. Students can now meet someone who is as close to a real-life client as possible.

This paper reports an empirical study of the first 15 months since the implementation of the method at HKU. In 2013 and 2014, 390 HKU PCLL students straddled over two academic years participated in interviewing exercises with the SCs. These SCs are lay persons trained to portray clients in a realistic manner by adopting the refined SC training programme ('the SC programme') of the Glasgow Graduate School of Law ('GGSL') in Scotland, available since 2006. Previous study has proven that SCs are able to assess law students' communicative competence as reliably and validly as, and yet more cost-effectively than, tutors (Barton *et al.*, 2006, pp. 20, 30 and 41). This paper extends the existing scholarship by further testing the hypotheses that: (1) apart from assessing students' communicative competence reliably and validly, SCs can also offer a valuable learning experience to law students and over repeated practices enhance their communication and interviewing skills; (2) although the SC programme can be transplanted to another jurisdiction, as shown in the case of HKU, the interview assessment and the learning experience of law students can be influenced by such cultural particularities as the use of language of the receiving jurisdiction. This paper will analyse data from 485 SC interviews held from February 2013 to April 2014 in HKU to test the above hypotheses. These interviews, conducted in English, involved 390 PCLL students.[1] The findings of this study may shed light for other law schools who may wish to customize the SC programme for their jurisdictions.

The next section of this paper will give an overview of the use of SCs in legal education in different parts of the world. Section III will briefly recapitulate the milestones of the curriculum reform to the HKU PCLL over the last decade leading to implementing various experiential learning tools including the SC programme, followed in Section IV by a chronological review of what took place over a 15-month period commencing from February 2013 when a pilot run of the SC programme at HKU PCLL was launched. Based upon the outcome of the pilot, a brief account of which will be presented in Section V, we decided to expand our SC programme. Section VI of this paper provides an analysis of the full run in the academic year 2013/14. Our findings not only confirm the reliability and validity of using SCs as teachers and assessors of interviewing skills, but also reveal the influence of cultural particularities over the performance and learning experience of law students. Section VII concludes the present study and on such a basis raises a number of further inquiries for legal educators to consider if they wish to adopt this innovative approach to legal education for their institutions.

II. Origin and development of standardized clients

Training lay persons to portray legal clients in assessing interviewing skills of law students, commonly known as standardized client interviews, has its origin in the clinical education of the medical schools in the US. Medical schools began using what they called standardized patients more than 40 years ago (Wallace, 1997, 2007, pp. xxiii–xxx). Actors were trained to assume the role of a patient, incorporating the patient's physical and mental profile to be interviewed by medical students (Cunningham, 1999, pp. 1960–1961; Barton *et al.*, 2006, pp. 2–3; Fry *et al.*,

2012, p. 138). The assessment tool was adapted in legal education from 1998 in the Effective Lawyer–Client Communication (ELCC) project, which was a collaboration by four law school clinics from the US and Australia.[2] New York Law School commenced its pilot project in 2001 to use SCs in a class on negotiating and counselling (Grosberg, 2001, 2004, 2006).

SCs have been used in high-stakes professional and licensing examinations since the mid-2000s when GGSL incorporated assessment through SC interviews as a prerequisite for obtaining a Diploma in Legal Practice in 2006; such a diploma is one of the requirements for receiving a legal practice licence in Scotland (Barton *et al.*, 2006, pp. 33–54; Cunningham, 2011, p. 505). In the US, since 2008, the Daniel Webster Scholar Honors Program ('DWS') provided by the University of New Hampshire School of Law has added SC interviews, based on the GGSL's model, as an additional assessment component to enhance their training on students' communication skills. Graduation from the DWS will lead to an admission to the bar without the need to sit the paper-based bar exam (Garvey & Zinkin, 2009; Garvey, 2010, 2013; IAALS, 2015). In 2011, the Solicitors Regulation Authority in England and Wales included SC interviews as one of the examination components in its Qualifying Lawyers Transfer Scheme ('QLTS') for licensing lawyers qualified in other jurisdictions who seek to practise in England and Wales (Fry *et al.*, 2012, 2013).

Also in 2011, the University of Northumbria Law School and The Law Society of Ireland made use of SCs as part of their law students' mandatory clinical work (Maharg, 2011) and continuing professional development programme (Standardized Client in Ireland, 2011) respectively. In Australia, the Graduate Diploma in Legal Practice course (similar to the Legal Practice Course in England and Wales) of the Australian National University introduced SC interviews to assess students' communication skills in 2012 (Mula *et al.*, 2012). The University of Adelaide's law school has also recently developed SC interviews into its programme (Chow & Ng, 2014, p. 166). HKU Faculty of Law is the first stop of the SC programme in Asia other than Australia. After HKU began its SC initiative in 2012, Kwansei Gakuin University Law School in Osaka, Japan also provided SC interviews for its students.

While most of the initiating professors of the above SC programmes have published their views and experience in implementing and evaluating their projects, empirical research on students' performance and evaluation has been in general lacking from the published works, apart from, as far as the authors know, the quantitative analyses contained in the article by Barton, Cunningham, Jones and Maharg on the GGSL's pilots (Barton *et al.*, 2006), another one by Fry, Crewe and Wakeford on Kaplan Law School's implementation of the QLTS (Fry *et al.*, 2012) and the recent report evaluating DWS issued by the Institute for the Advancement of the American Legal System (IAALS, 2015). Such an omission is one of the major differences between "what medical educators have done in terms of the quality and quantity of empirical research on methods of assessing professional competence and what legal educators have done, or more specially, not done" (Grosberg, 2006, p. 870). Therefore the much needed aim of this paper is to fill such a gap by contributing empirical analyses of using SCs as an assessment and teaching method in legal education. While a comprehensive comparative study with SCs used in other parts of the world is not a primary objective of this paper, it will, where applicable, briefly compare such previously published data with findings at HKU.[3]

III. A belated birth: experiential learning in legal education and SCs in HKU

A unified qualification preparing students for vocational training as trainee solicitors or pupil barristers in Hong Kong, the PCLL has always been housed within a university department. It was thought to be sensible to provide "an intellectually challenging continuum between the LLB and PCLL, rather than an abrupt move to an arid practical training course" (Willoughby, 1999, p. 42) when the first and then only law school in Hong Kong was set up at HKU in 1969 with its first PCLL cohort of about 40 graduates ready to join the legal profession as articled clerks or pupils four years later. At that time, the PCLL was "partly didactic" and "only partly practical" (Evans, 1989, p. 25), rather heavily loaded with substantive law. The HKU monopoly came to an end in 1991. Since 2006, Hong Kong has had three law schools.

Various attempts in the HKU PCLL to bridge the gap between the academic stage of legal education and the practical stage had been made over its first three decades but they were generally piecemeal. Little reform had actually taken place. Initiated by the Law Society of Hong Kong, the year 2001 saw a landmark review of legal education and training commissioned by the Hong Kong Government, which led to major curriculum reform of the HKU PCLL. Starting at a modest scale, it had taken seven years to get to a renovated PCLL at HKU. As illustrated in Figures 1 and 2 below, the new curriculum is designed and constructed on a

Problem solving Document analysis Issue identification Legal research		
Research memo writing	*Litigation-specific*	*Transaction-specific*
Advice writing	Pleadings drafting	Document drafting
Pleadings drafting	Affidavit drafting	Letter writing
Affidavit drafting	Opinion writing	Interviewing
Interviewing	Advocacy (non-trial and trial)	Negotiation/Mediation
Conferencing	Interviewing/Conferencing	
Advocacy (non-trial)	Negotiation/Mediation	
File and case management	Use of Chinese language in legal practice	
Professional ethics and values		

Figure 1. HKU PCLL – Skills set

Core Practice Areas	*Elective Practice Areas*	
Civil Litigation	*Litigation-specific*	*Transaction-specific*
Criminal Litigation	Commercial Dispute Resolution	Drafting Commercial Agreements
Corporate & Commercial Transactions	Matrimonial Practice and Procedure	Listed Companies
Property Transactions I	Personal Injury Litigation	Property Transactions II
	Property Litigation	Wills, Trusts and Estate Planning
	Trial Advocacy	Employment Law and Practice
		China Practice
	Use of Chinese in Legal Practice	
Professional Practice and Management		

Figure 2. HKU PCLL – Subject practice areas

better balanced tripod of knowledge, skills and professional ethics, with a degree of specialization through electives.

In addition, the new HKU PCLL makes use of case files taken or adapted from real cases, rather than isolated and unconnected hypotheticals, in most of its courses to allow students to go through the entire transaction or process (or a truncated part or truncated parts of it) and carry out certain designated lawyering tasks.

Despite these moves, the majority of HKU PCLL students still found it difficult in their transition from the qualifying law degree to the PCLL (Jen, 2009), particularly in relation to the necessary change in their mind-sets from studying *about* the law to *applying* the law. In addition, the graduate surveys conducted by the Law Society over the years informed us of the need for greater stress on communication skills training. In our search for ways to further improve the HKU PCLL, we have turned our eyes to the common call for a combination of various learning methods with increasing emphasis on experiential learning, including learning in real life and learning by realistic simulations, with or without the aid of technology. The SC programme is one among these.

IV. A quick growth: seven sessions of 600 interviews in 15 months

The local circumstances make it difficult for law students in Hong Kong to acquire such soft skills as communication skills with clients by learning in real life through internships (Chow & Tiba, 2013). Apart from a total of about 240 locally-bred LLB graduates from the three law schools each year, there is a diverse mix of other PCLL applicants of other qualifying law degrees. These include returnees from overseas after undertaking a law degree in another common-law jurisdiction, Hong Kong residents completing law studies locally via external programmes such as the LLB from the University of London or from the Manchester Metropolitan University and the Common Professional Examination of England and Wales. In addition, all three law schools now offer and run their own Juris Doctor programme. In rare cases a qualified lawyer in an overseas jurisdiction chooses to take the PCLL in order to practise Hong Kong law. In each of the last three years, consolidated data from the three law school show that over 1,300[4] applicants (some of them nevertheless apply to more than one provider) have competed for a total of about 650 PCLL places, full-time and part-time.

On the other hand, with more than 820 registered law firms in Hong Kong, a vast majority of which are either sole proprietorships or with no more than two partners[5] and a significant number of those sole practitioners do not even employ any other legally qualified persons,[6] it is entirely unrealistic to expect a sufficient number of internships for law students. An optional clinical course running under resource and other constraints can hardly alleviate the concern in any significant way (Chow & Tiba, 2013). The conventional way of training through simulated interviews with legally qualified tutors or, sometimes, classmates, playing the role is quite different from 'doing the real thing' with real clients lay to the law. The SC programme seems to be the best available solution in this far from perfect world, providing students with realistic experience which mimics what they will encounter in their real-life legal practice in future.

In the course of planning and preparation for the pilot programme in the spring semester of 2012/13, advice was sought from overseas experts and trainers. Intensive coaching led by experienced trainers from the UK was provided for the first group of 10 SCs recruited. Wills, Trusts and Estate Planning ('WTEP'), one of the HKU PCLL electives, was chosen as the base for the pilot. Sixty-four students enrolled to the elective and engaged themselves in two rounds of interviews, a practice towards the end of February followed by an assessment in mid-March.

The results of the pilot programme will be outlined in Sections V and VI. Suffice to say, feedback from students on the pilot was predominantly positive. The support for extending the SC programme to the core subjects was overwhelming.

Table 1. *Number of interviews done via the SC programme at HKU PCLL (February 2013–April 2014)*

Date	Course	Number of interviews
February 2013	WTEP	63 (practice)
March 2013		64 (assessment)
November, December 2013	Civil Lit.	326 (practice)
February 2014	WTEP	59 (practice)
March 2014		59 (assessment)
April 2014	ELP	29(assessment)
Total		600

During the academic year 2013/14, we repeated the cycle for WTEP and expanded the SC programme to Civil Litigation ('Civil Lit.'), a core subject in the PCLL in the fall semester. More than 320 students, full-time and part-time, participated in a practice exercise. Given the increase in the number of students involved, it required two sessions to complete all interviews in each of the full-time and part-time cohorts even with a rapidly expanded pool of 30 SCs after an amazingly fast growth of the idea through word of mouth by some of our first SCs. In addition to WTEP, students in the Employment Law and Practice elective ('ELP') joined in. Each of the 29 students enrolled to the ELP elective was required to do an interviewing assessment with an SC. As Table 1 shows, our SC programme had run seven sessions of 600 interviews completed in just about 15 months since its first inception.

Compared with our counterparts in Scotland and Australia,[7] Hong Kong had a late start but is catching up at a most remarkable speed.

V. A trial run in an elective course in 2012–13

The pilot SC programme at HKU PCLL was launched in the spring semester of 2013. Over two weeks, students enrolled to the WTEP elective interviewed two different SCs, one at a time in a practice and in a subsequent assessment, under time constraints and with a view to amending or drafting a will for the client. Prior to the actual interviews with student lawyers, we assured the reliability and validity of SCs' assessment by running over 10 standardization exercises with the recruited SCs during a three-day training workshop, at the end of which the trainers were satisfied that the SCs were able to match the HKU's standard in assessing communication competence of student lawyers according to the assessment form and criteria refined by GGSL (Barton *et al.*, 2006). More particulars of such standardization exercises will be described in Section VI. During the actual interviews with student lawyers, SCs were required to provide a mark on the assessment form according to a five-point scale for each of the eight criteria. The criteria are:

(1) the greeting and introduction by the student lawyer was appropriate;
(2) I felt the student lawyer listened to me;
(3) the student lawyer's approach to questioning was helpful;
(4) the student lawyer accurately summarized my situation;
(5) I understood what the student lawyer was saying;
(6) I felt comfortable with the student lawyer;
(7) I would feel confident with the student lawyer dealing with my situation; and
(8) if I had a new legal problem I would come back to this student lawyer.

Criteria 1, 6 and 7 relate to the general rapport of the interviewing session, criteria 2–5 concern the information exchange that took place during the interview and the last criterion represents an overall customer satisfaction level (Chow & Ng, 2014, p. 170). A passing score is 50% of the total marks, i.e. 20 marks. The higher the score achieved by a student, the higher the level of communicative competence he/she attained. On top of grading students' ability according to such a five-point scale, SCs will, if

Table 2. *Analysis of SCs' grading of practice session (26 February 2013) (N = 63)*

	Score						
Criteria	1	2	3	4	5	*M*	*SD*
(1) Appropriate intro and greeting	3	20	31	9	0	2.73	0.761
(2) Felt listened	0	22	27	13	1	2.89	0.779
(3) Helpful questioning	3	29	25	5	1	2.56	0.774
(4) Accurate summary	18	7	29	9	0	2.44	1.067
(5) Understood what lawyer said	2	21	31	8	0	2.73	0.723
(6) Comfortable with lawyer	0	21	33	9	0	2.81	0.664
(7) Felt confident with lawyer	7	32	16	8	0	2.41	0.849
(8) Would come back again	10	33	15	5	0	2.25	0.816
Overall	50% pass					2.60	

Note: N = Sample size; M = Mean; SD = Standard Deviation.

necessary, give brief written comments on students' performance or feedback as to which of the above eight areas the students need to improve.

In this pilot, the teacher deliberately gave no briefing before the practice round apart from urging the students to go through the eight assessment criteria and the rubrics themselves. A review session was, however, conducted in the week following the formative assessment, mainly summarizing the SCs' feedback on student performance in the practice session with reference to those criteria and rubrics. In addition, each student was given the hyperlink to his or her own video-recorded performance and a copy of the comment sheet filled out by the SC. Approximately a week later, students were assessed summatively. Tables 2 and 3 show and compare the practice and assessment results of the students in this pilot.

From these tables, we arrive at the following observations.

(1) Overall improvement: only 50% of students attained the passing score of 20 or above in the practice session but at the actual assessment most of them (89%) passed.

Table 3. *Analysis of SCs' grading of assessment session (12 March 2013) (N = 64)*

	Score						
Criteria	1	2	3	4	5	*M*	*SD*
(1) Appropriate intro and greeting	2	14	28	20	0	3.02	0.820
(2) Felt listened	0	9	33	19	3	3.25	0.751
(3) Helpful questioning	0	10	30	23	1	3.23	0.724
(4) Accurate summary	2	2	35	22	3	3.31	0.809
(5) Understood what lawyer said	0	8	46	9	1	3.05	0.571
(6) Comfortable with lawyer	0	13	37	14	0	3.00	0.661
(7) Felt confident with lawyer	0	10	40	14	0	3.05	0.623
(8) Would come back again	0	17	35	12	0	2.91	0.678
Overall	89% pass					3.10	

Note: N = Sample size; M = Mean; SD = Standard Deviation.

(2) Students' communicative competence level on average rose from the non-competent/borderline competent level (mean scores from 2.25 to 2.89) in the practice session, to a competent/marginally very competent level (mean item score from 2.91 to 3.31) at the actual assessment.
(3) Significant improvement (21%) was shown in the information exchange criteria 2–5 (the hard skills). In particular, students' performance in criterion 4 (The student lawyer accurately summarized my situation) boosted from a mean score of 2.44 during the practice interview to 3.31 during the actual assessment.
(4) In contrast, student lawyers improved to a lesser extent (17%) in the rapport and impression criteria 1, 6, 7 and 8 (the soft skills).
(5) In both sessions, criterion 8 (If I had a new legal problem I would come back to this student lawyer) stood out as the weakest link.

From comparing the mean scores of this relatively small cohort in the practice and assessment sessions, we are able to preliminarily observe that, with the rather minimal 'coaching' done by the subject teacher, SCs are not only able to assess communicative competence of law students, but also become teachers of communication skills. Students can learn experientially through interviewing the SCs and improve their ability to approach client interviews as they practise.

VI. A fuller run in a compulsory course and two electives in 2013–14

After the trial run, we solicited students' views as to whether they would support the extension of the SC programme to the core subjects of PCLL. Of the 41 respondents, more than 75% of them agreed that the interviews enhanced their communicative competence. Some of those who expressed disagreement commented that enhancement in communicative competence could be better achieved if individual feedback sessions could be held between SCs and the students.[8] Yet, more than 90% of them welcomed the extension of the SC programme to the core subjects. One compulsory course (Civil Lit.) and two electives (WTEP and ELP) were chosen as the target courses for the academic year 2013/14.

The entire cohort of 326 students, representing 251 full-time and 75 part-time students, participated in the practice interview sessions with SCs in Civil Lit. The case for the interview concerned a negligence claim, against which the student lawyer acted for the defendant. Specifically, the claim was lodged by a newly married woman against a catering company which she had engaged to arrange her wedding banquet and prepare a six-tier wedding cake. The wedding cake collapsed during the ceremony and spoiled the party. The SC acted as an experienced patisserie chef of the defendant company and was responsible for making the cake. For the purposes of defending the case, the chef was asked by her/his boss to give a witness statement. The chef had never been interviewed by a lawyer before and therefore was nervous and afraid of losing his/her job if something wrong was said. The interview was scheduled to take place in late November (for the full-time students) and early December, 2013 (for the part-time students), and students had been working through the case since the beginning of the semester in September and had completed such tasks as pleadings drafting and discovery based on such a case scenario. Also different from the pilot, the teacher this time gave a briefing before this formative assessment. Students were also showed two videos of students' performance from the pilot, although the contexts and purposes of the interviews were not the same.

Sixteen SCs were recruited to be interviewed by the student lawyers.[9] Depending on their availability, each SC had 10–27 students allocated randomly for interview. To ensure the SCs became familiar with the scenario, the required acting techniques and the assessment standard, training sessions took place at HKU over three days in October 2013, modelled on the inaugural training in February 2013. The training sessions were divided into three parts, namely general role-playing training, familiarization and practice of scenarios and scripts, and assessment training and standardization. The most important component of the training was the numerous practice interviews between SCs and our faculty colleagues. In these interviews, our faculty members acted as the student lawyers to interview the SCs according to the given scenario. While one of the SCs was being interviewed, he/she, together with the remaining SCs and the trainers (faculty members who sat through and participated in the inaugural training) assessed the interviewing lawyer and marked them on their own assessment forms. After each practice interview, trainers compared the SCs' scores with those of the trainers and discussed the similarities and divergences among them so that the SCs would know to what extent they had been following the HKU's standard in scoring the eight-criteria assessment form. These training activities were aimed at ensuring validity and reliability of using SCs for assessing the communicative competence of law students, particularly since, and when, the SC programme is being transferred across jurisdictions. At the end of eight rounds of practice interviews, it was found that the SCs' scores by and large converged with the trainers' ratings. We tested the consistency between SCs' and tutors' ratings using Cronbach's Alpha, as shown in Table 4. The results show a statistically acceptable level of consistency in most (six out of eight) of the practice interviews. Low

Table 4. *Reliability (internal consistency) of SCs' marking in eight mock interviews held during the three-day training (in October 2013)*

Mock interview	*N*	*M*	*SD*	Internal consistency (Cronbach's Alpha[a])
1	15	3.53	0.42	0.234
2	15	2.24	0.44	0.868
3	15	3.39	0.55	0.910
4	15	2.73	0.65	0.933
5	15	4.22	0.34	0.430
6	17	3.45	0.41	0.987
7	17	2.01	0.29	0.976
8	17	2.32	0.32	0.951

Note: *N* = Sample size; *M* = Mean; *SD* = Standard Deviation. [a]Reliability of SCs' ratings was tested by Cronbach's Alpha, for which a cut-off of 0.70 or above can be regarded as an acceptable value of the coefficient. Higher Cronbach's Alpha indicates an increasing reliability (Cronbach & Shavelson, 2004, p. 391).

consistency of 0.234 in the first interview was not surprising as that was the first practice. The relatively low value of 0.43 shown in the fifth interview did not worry us too much because the main divergence was in whether the lawyer's overall performance was very good (score of 4) or excellent (score of 5), as opposed to that in rating a pass versus a failing performance, or a fair versus a good performance. The results also show, despite the fact that the SC group had doubled in size, that a larger group of SCs after proper training were still able to articulate information as a lay client in a relatively consistent way and able to assess an interviewer as validly and reliably as tutors do in examining the communicative competence of a student lawyer.

VI.1. Overall student performance

The actual interviewing exercise took place on 20–21 November and 2–3 December 2013. The mean scores in different criteria constituting the communicative competence of all students in the SC practice interview session of Civil Lit. are summarized in Table 5. From the table, we can observe that:

(1) nearly 59% of the 326-student cohort passed in their interview exercise with SCs, which is not much different from the 50% passing rate of a smaller cohort (63 students) in the trial run at their first attempt;
(2) students performed better in criteria 5 (the client understood what the lawyer said; mean score: 3.13) and 2 (the client felt that the lawyer listened to him/her; mean score: 3.06). The worst performed aspects were criteria 4 (the lawyer accurately summarized client's instructions; mean score: 1.97), 8 (the client felt that he/she would come back to the lawyer; mean score: 2.58) and 1 (the lawyer greeted the client appropriately; mean score: 2.74). The two lists are quite similar to those compiled from the results of the practice session of the trial run;

Table 5. *Analysis of SCs' grading of SC practice interview session in Civil Lit. (21–22 November and 2–3 December 2013) (N = 326)*

	Score						
Criteria	1	2	3	4	5	*M*	*SD*
(1) Appropriate intro and greeting	18	117	125	64	2	2.74	0.857
(2) Felt listened	4	61	174	85	2	3.06	0.721
(3) Helpful questioning	6	97	167	53	3	2.85	0.741
(4) Accurate summary	165	47	73	41	0	1.97	1.112
(5) Understood what lawyer said	1	31	220	72	2	3.13	0.580
(6) Comfortable with lawyer	8	99	147	68	4	2.97	1.753
(7) Felt confident with lawyer	9	107	161	48	1	2.77	0.740
(8) Would come back again	36	121	116	50	3	2.58	0.911
Overall	59% pass					2.76	

Note: *N* = Sample size; *M* = Mean; *SD* = Standard Deviation.

Table 6. *Independent-samples* t-*test results between scores obtained by female and male students in SC practice interview session in Civil Lit. (21–22 November and 2–3 December 2013) (N = 326)*

	Female ($N = 197$)		Male ($N = 129$)			
Criteria	*M*	*SD*	*M*	*SD*	*df*	*t*-test
(1) Appropriate intro and greeting	2.83	0.83	2.60	0.88	324	2.445*
(2) Felt listened	3.18	0.72	2.88	0.69	324	3.670***
(5) Understood what lawyer said	3.20	0.59	3.03	0.56	283	2.589**
(8) Would come back again	2.67	0.93	2.44	0.76	324	2.226*

Note: N = Sample size; M = Mean; SD = Standard Deviation. $^{*}p < 0.05$; $^{**}p < 0.01$; $^{***}p < 0.001$.

(3) such a similar pattern of scores reveals and supports the belief that: law students in Hong Kong generally do better in hard skills such as listening to and recording instructions and articulating advice; however, there is room for improvement in their soft skills such as offering appropriate greetings to clients and making the clients feel relaxed and comfortable, irrespective of whether a briefing before they are put into practice has been carried out.

VI.2. Possible factors underpinning students' performance – study mode, educational background and gender

Apart from understanding the overall performance of Hong Kong law students in interviewing skills and communicative competence, we are equally, if not more interested in exploring possible factors that may have underpinned such a performance. A number of factors were hypothesized to have an impact on the final scores of students in the SC exercise, namely, study mode, educational background and gender of the students. Prior to the exercise, we anticipated that: (a) female students would generally be better at client communication than male students; (b) full-time students would score higher marks than part-time students who might be less well prepared for the exercise due to their day-time jobs; and (c) students with overseas under graduate experience would be communicatively more able than local Hong Kong graduates.

Independent-samples *t*-tests were run to analyse the relationship between these factors and the performance of individual items.[10] It is found that female students did perform better than male students, especially in criteria 1, 2, 5 and 8

Table 7. *Independent-samples* t-*test results between scores obtained by full-time and part-time students in SC practice interview session in Civil Lit. (21–22 November and 2–3 December 2013) (N = 326)*

	FT ($N = 251$)		PT ($N = 75$)			
Criteria	*M*	*SD*	*M*	*SD*	*df*	*t*-test
(5) Understood what lawyer said	3.17	0.57	3.00	0.59	118	2.214*

Note: N = Sample size; M = Mean; SD = Standard Deviation; FT = Full-time students; PT = Part-time students. $^{*}p < 0.05$.

(see Table 6 below). Women's apparent advantage was also shown by the higher pass rate in the results of Objective Structured Clinical Examination ('OSCE'), which formed one of the three key tests for passing the QLTS held in the UK in 2011. In OSCE, a candidate interviews an SC, followed by preparing an attendance note and making an oral presentation (Fry *et al.*, 2012, p. 144).[11] In relation to study-mode, contrary to our expectations, full-time students did not outperform their part-time counterparts in most of the items, except in criterion 5 [$t(118) = 2.214$, $p = 0.029$], i.e. to get the client to understand what they said, as shown in Table 7. On the other hand, all students with an overseas undergraduate law degree passed the exercise while 3.1% of Hong Kong graduates failed. The above analysis confirms our hypotheses that female students and students with experience of study overseas perform better in handling an initial face-to-face interview with clients. Yet, full-time students do not necessarily have a clear advantage over their part-time classmates in handling issues in client communication. The part-timers' lack of time for preparation for the exercise due to day-time engagements could possibly be compensated for by the fact that they are in general more mature in age and have more real-life working experience in dealing with people.

VI.3. Language – an historical and cultural particularity of an Asian common-law jurisdiction

We also hypothesized language background as a major factor that might have an impact on the interview ratings scored by the students due to the historical and cultural particularities of Hong Kong, a former British colony, in its use of language in legal education and practice. Law students in Hong Kong learned the law and are assessed on their legal knowledge in English, yet the majority of them are Chinese by ethnic origin and converse in Cantonese (a major dialect of Guangdong Province in Southern China) in social life. Upon graduation and completion of traineeship, lawyers in Hong Kong communicate with clients, who are predominantly Chinese, in both Cantonese and English, and sometimes (and indeed more and more) in Mandarin. Yet, most of the practitioners' written correspondences with law firms, counsels, regulators, law enforcement agencies, the courts and their clients are in English. Such an interactive relationship among these three spoken languages in the workplace is not uncommon for the service industry in Hong Kong.[12] Within the cohort of law students in the present research, all their SC interviews were conducted in English as HKU's prescribed medium of instruction. Some 22% of them earned their qualifying law degrees from overseas universities, primarily in the UK, and the rest of them were educated in Hong Kong. We have seen in the preceding paragraph that overseas graduates performed relatively better in certain aspects of a client interview. They are in a more advantageous position in interviewing the SCs in English possibly because of their higher degree of exposure in daily communication in English as compared with local graduates.

Another equally, if not more important variable is the language background of SCs. Four of our 16 SCs hired in the Civil Lit. are native English speakers ('English-speaking SCs'), while all others are Chinese but they speak English fluently

Table 8. *Independent-samples* t*-test results between scores given by Chinese- and English-speaking SCs in Civil Lit. (21–22 November and 2–3 December 2013) (N = 326)*

	Chinese-speaking SCs			English-speaking SCs				
Criteria	*N*	*M*	*SD*	*N*	*M*	*SD*	*df*	*t*-test
Local graduates (185/70)	185	2.65	0.56	70	2.92	0.57	252	−3.40**
Overseas graduates (55/17)	55	2.79	0.68	17	3.12	0.64	28	−1.84

Note: N = Sample size; M = Mean; SD = Standard Deviation. $^{**}p < 0.01$.

as their second language ('Chinese-speaking SCs'). In fact such a combination of SCs mirrors a similar client-mix of a lawyer in practice in Hong Kong. Our enquiry is: would the language background of the students and SCs affect the ratings scored by the students in their SC interviews? And if so, in what way? For example, would a Hong Kong student be disadvantaged if he/she interviewed a native English-speaking client rather than a Chinese one? Our major concern is whether one's second language as the main legal language of the place would have any impact on assessing law students' communicative competence.

Independent-samples *t*-tests were run in order to investigate the impact of these variables on students' results, as shown in Table 8. While the perception might be that English-speaking SCs were more sensitive and strict in rating other's ability to communicate in English, our analyses, on the contrary, reveal that they tend to be more lenient in grading both overseas and local graduates. As shown in Table 8, the mean scores obtained by local graduates from Chinese-speaking SCs and English-speaking SCs are 2.65 and 2.92, respectively. Such a difference is considered statistically significant. The mean scores rated by Chinese-speaking SCs and English-speaking SCs on overseas graduates are 2.79 and 3.12, respectively. Such a difference is not regarded as statistically significant because the *t*-test results might have been affected by the relatively small sample size of overseas graduates assessed by English-speaking SCs (17 students). Therefore, it would not be unreasonable to expect that a statistically more significant difference could be observed if the sample size was bigger. From the above analysis we are able to say that using English as a medium of interview would possibly create certain advantaged and disadvantaged groups in the assessment of communicative competence, as illustrated in the matrix shown in Table 9. An overseas law graduate may be in the most advantageous position if they were to interview an English-speaking SC; a local graduate may have the least relative advantage in front of a Chinese-speaking SC. These results in a certain way echoed the analyses of candidates' results in OSCE of

Table 9. *Matrix of relative advantage in SCs' assessment*

	Chinese SC	English-speaking SC
Local graduates	Likely least advantage	Average
Overseas graduates	Average	Likely most advantage

QLTS conducted in 2011 in the UK with respect to the significance of language in SC assessments. Statistical analysis shows that all candidates speaking English as the first language passed the OSCE while only 71% of those with a first language other than English passed it (Fry *et al.*, 2012, p. 143).[13]

VI.4. Experiential learning in SC interviews across disciplines

We have seen in Section V that students on the WTEP course in 2012–13 learned from the SC interviews during the practice session and obtained better ratings in the subsequent assessment under a similar context. Could communication skills learned from one practice area be transferred and applied to another or even perhaps with better and enhanced performance? We address this enquiry by tracking the performance of 32 students who took part in the Civil Lit. practice session in the first semester of the academic year 2013–14 and subsequently enrolled for WTEP or ELP in the second semester where they would attend at least one more SC interview. The mean scores awarded to these 32 students in their Civil Lit. interviews and in their WTEP/ELP interviews were statistically compared. Results reveal that statistically significant improvement was demonstrated by the students in performing criteria 1 (the lawyer greeted the client appropriately), 2 (the client felt the student lawyer listened to him/her), 4 (the lawyer accurately summarized the client's instructions) and 7 (the client felt confident with the lawyer dealing with his/her situation). This confirms our hypothesis that SCs are also teachers of communication skills; through them students can learn experientially and improve their ability to approach client interviews with better client care, sensitivity and structure even across different areas of legal practice (Table 10).[14]

VI.5. Students' evaluation of learning experience from SC

While we are able to see students learn and improve their performance as reflected in their score sheets, do they feel the same benefit? Since there is no major scholarship in the field that reports students' feedback to the SC programme, we attempt to understand students' evaluation of the SC programme and, more importantly, to investigate how students from different backgrounds perceive this programme differently. To

Table 10. *Paired-sample* t-*test result between students' performance in SC practice sessions of Civil Lit. (21–22 November and 2–3 December 2013) and WTEP/ELP (11 February 2014 and 2 May 2014)* (N = 32)

	CL		WTEP/ELP			
Criteria	*M*	*SD*	*M*	*SD*	*df*	*t*-test
(1) Appropriate intro and greeting	2.72	0.77	3.44	0.91	31	3.75**
(2) Felt listened	3.19	0.64	3.72	0.63	31	−3.42*
(4) Accurate summary	1.94	1.01	3.09	1.12	31	−3.88**
(7) Felt confident with lawyer	2.94	0.84	3.25	0.76	31	−2.20*
Average score	2.80	0.51	3.32	0.59	31	−3.75**

Note: N = Sample size; M = Mean; SD = Standard Deviation. $^{*}p < 0.05$; $^{**}p < 0.01$.

solicit their feedback on how the SC programme helped them learn, we conducted a self-administered anonymous survey to the students. Students were asked to fill out a questionnaire of eight open-ended questions and 21 questions, through which they evaluated each aspect of their lawyering skills and learning experience. The evaluation form is divided into four parts. Part A asks specifically if the students feel that the SC programme enhances their communicative ability in client interviews. Part B asks more general questions to understand if students feel that the SC programme makes them learn more enjoyably and be better prepared to be a practising lawyer. Both parts use a Likert scale from 1 (Strongly Disagree) to 5 (Strongly Agree). Part C asks students certain open-ended questions for their opinion on the strengths and weaknesses of the SC programme as a part of their legal learning. Part D asks for students' personal background so that we can understand how different groups of students react to these questions. Specifically, we seek information as to their gender, the university where their first law degree was earned, and their first spoken language. Of the entire 326 student-cohort, 177 students returned their completed evaluation forms.[15]

Overall evaluation from students is positive and encouraging (see Table 11). On average students give a 3.5–4 to most of the questions asked in both Part A and Part B of the questionnaire, indicating their general recognition of the effectiveness of the SC programme in enhancing their ability to communicate with clients and their interest in learning, and in making them better prepared for their future lawyering career. Due to the constraints of space in this paper, we focus our analyses only on questions contained in Part A of the evaluation, which more specifically relate to how students felt regarding whether their skills and abilities in client communication were improved through the SC programme. In Part A, questions concerning enhancement of ability of attentive listening, questioning and clear explanation received relatively higher scores (approximately 3.7 points). In contrast, students awarded relatively lower scores (approximately 3.4–3.5 points) to questions concerning whether the SC

Table 11. *Results of students' evaluation of learning experience of SC programme in Civil Lit.* (N = *177)*

Questions	*M*	*SD*
Part A – SCs programme enhanced students skills/abilities in:		
(A1) attentive listening	3.70	0.87
(A2) questioning clients	3.72	0.85
(A3) summarizing information	3.58	0.88
(A4) explaining clearly	3.72	0.85
(A5) problem-solving	3.44	0.91
(A6) communication competence	3.70	0.85
(A7) building rapport and trust with client	3.58	0.92
(A8) understanding how clients feel	3.61	0.99
(A9) demonstrating empathy towards clients	3.53	1.01
(A10) demonstrating respect towards clients	3.56	0.92
Overall mean	3.61	

Note: *N* = Sample size; *M* = Mean; *SD* = Standard Deviation.

Table 12. *Independent-samples* t*-test results between female and male students' evaluation of learning experience of SC programme in Civil Lit.*

	Female ($N = 98$)		Male ($N = 59$)			
Criteria	M	SD	M	SD	df	t-test
(A2) questioning	3.88	0.61	3.51	1.07	81	2.415*
(A7) building rapport and trust	3.71	0.75	3.34	1.14	89	2.234*
(A9) demonstrating empathy	3.71	0.90	3.24	1.12	103	2.755**
(A10) demonstrating respect	3.72	0.81	3.34	1.04	100	2.406*

Note: N = Sample size; M = Mean; SD = Standard Deviation. *$p < 0.05$; **$p < 0.01$.

programme strengthened students' problem solving skills and their ability to demonstrate empathy and respect towards clients. Many of them suggested that such skills could be further sharpened if SCs could give oral feedback immediately after the interviews.[16] Similar to how we analyse students' ratings in SC interviews, we hypothesized that differences in perception of the learning experience could be observed from students' gender, educational and language background.

Independent-samples t-tests were again run against the evaluation results. The findings show that female students evaluated the SC programme more favourably than male students, as shown in Table 12, in terms of enhancing their questioning skills and their abilities in building rapport and trust with clients, as well as in demonstrating empathy and respect towards them. Of the 153 valid responses on their first spoken language, 129 students speak Cantonese, 14 speak English, nine speak Mandarin and the remaining student spoke another dialect. Since the difference

Table 13. *Means of evaluation of learning experience of SC programme in Civil Lit. scored by Mandarin speaker, Cantonese speaker and English speaker*

	MS ($N = 9$)		CS ($N = 129$)		ES ($N = 14$)	
Criteria	M	SD	M	SD	M	SD
Part A – SCs enhanced students skills/abilities in:						
(A1) listening	3.78	0.91	3.77	0.81	3.14	1.10
(A2) questioning	3.89	0.78	3.78	0.97	3.21	1.12
(A3) summarizing client's situation	3.78	0.83	3.65	0.83	3.00	1.04
(A4) explanation	3.89	0.93	3.81	0.76	2.86	0.95
(A5) problem solving	3.67	0.87	3.49	0.88	2.93	1.07
(A6) communication competence	3.67	0.87	3.74	0.82	3.21	1.05
(A7) building rapport and trust	3.56	1.01	3.61	0.90	3.14	1.17
(A8) understanding how clients feel	3.67	0.87	3.64	1.01	3.29	1.14
(A9) demonstrating empathy	3.44	1.01	3.58	1.00	3.21	1.12
(A10) demonstrating respect	3.78	0.83	3.60	0.91	3.21	1.12
Overall means	3.71		3.67		3.12	

Note: N = Sample size; M = Mean; SD = Standard Deviation; MS = Mandarin speaker; CS = Cantonese speaker; ES = English speaker.

between the sample sizes of different language groups is rather large, only simple comparison of means instead of another independent-samples *t*-test was carried out. As shown in Table 13, students who speak Mandarin as their first language on average rated seven out of the 10 questions (Questions A1–A5, A8 and A10) more favourably than their classmates, hence indicating a more rewarding learning experience from the SC interviews. Apart from again confirming our hypothesis that when a non-mother-tongue language is used as a medium for the SC programme it would create divergence not only in students' performance but also their personal experience of the experiential learning process, two other note-worthy observations can be drawn. Although the sample sizes of Mandarin-speaking students and Cantonese-speaking students differ greatly (9:129), the margin of their mean scores to each question is indeed small. They consider the effectiveness of the SC programme by and large in a similar way. In contrast, although the sample sizes of English-speaking students and Mandarin-speaking students are more or less the same (14:9), the divergence in their perceived value of the SC programme is significant. Such phenomenon could be explained by the fact that most, if not all, of the Mandarin-speaking students were educated in Mainland China prior to university education and were much less exposed to experience in English verbal communication while their Cantonese-speaking Hong Kong students began learning English as a second language in their early childhood. They might appreciate better the relevance and importance of mastering English interviews. It would be worthwhile to further investigate if such phenomenon could be found in other jurisdictions of parallel socio-lingual characteristics, where English is a second language and yet the major medium of legal education.

VII. Conclusion – simulated clients as a long-term solution?

As the first law school in Hong Kong and one of the earliest law schools among the former British colonies in the Far East, the HKU Faculty of Law has adopted the liberal studies approach of British universities in studying law and did not do much experiential learning until fairly recently. Yet in the last decade, it has caught up quickly by establishing a law clinic and introducing a number of other initiatives, the SC programme being one of them. Previous scholarship on the first SC programme in GGSL has proven that SCs are as reliable and valid as tutors, and yet less costly, for assessing the communicative competence of law students. Building upon the successful experience in the UK, the HKU PCLL imported the SC programme in the academic year of 2012–13 and has run more than 600 interview exercises for more than 300 PCLL students since then. This paper reports the promising results of the transplantation of this innovative approach to legal education in Hong Kong. It extends previous scholarship by not only confirming the ability of the SCs to assess students' communicative competence in a client interview in a different jurisdiction, but also demonstrating their ability in offering valuable experiential learning outcomes to students. This paper also, for the first time, attempts to analyse and report the relationship between students' background, their spoken language in particular, and their communicative competence as well as their self-perceived learning experience under a particular cultural and linguistic context of an Asian common-law jurisdiction. A number of important observations in relation to learning, teaching and assessment of communication and interviewing skills of law students can be made from the 15-month operation of the SC programme at HKU and the empirical analysis thereof.

(1) The SCs in Hong Kong are, similar to their counterparts in the UK, reliable and valid assessors of the communicative competence of law students at HKU, as confirmed by the results of a standardization exercise. Therefore it is proven that such an innovative approach to assessing students' communicative competence can be successfully transferred across continents and institutions.
(2) The SC programme offers substantial experiential learning to students. Students benefit from interviewing an SC and perform better when they meet another SC on a subsequent occasion. Such enhancement in communicative competence has been proven not only in students having interviewed SCs twice in the same course under a similar fact scenario, but also in those who interviewed different SCs in two different courses under totally different sets of facts. It shows that communication skills learnt by students from interviewing an SC can be successfully transferred and applied across different areas of legal practice. The SCs' role as teachers in communicative competence through such an experiential learning environment should be emphasized as being as important as, if not more important than, their ability and role as assessors.
(3) It is also found that students' background, in particular their educational and language background, has a bearing on their performance in interviews and their self-perceived benefits of the SC programme. Local and overseas law graduates differed in performance in interviews with SCs of different native languages. The findings show that local graduates may be disadvantaged when English, as their second language, is used as the medium of SCs interview. On the other hand, the English-speaking SCs tend to be more lenient in marking, regardless of students' language background, than SCs whose mother tongue is Chinese.
(4) Despite the overall positive evaluation of the learning experience, students' background again has a bearing on students' self-perceived learning benefits from SCs' interviews. Female students tend to evaluate the experience more favourably than male students. More importantly, language, again, differentiates the level of satisfaction. Students who speak Mandarin as their first language, primarily educated in Mainland China and who started to learn English later than their Cantonese-speaking Hong Kong classmates, tend to find the learning experience most rewarding.

These findings confirm our hypotheses that a lay client, with proper training, can act as a valid assessor as well as an effective teacher of communication skills in legal education.

The SC programme fills an important gap in legal education where client interviewing skills cannot be satisfactorily and effectively taught and assessed because of various limitations and constraints. However, when transplanting this approach as a long-term solution for teaching communication skills to students in an Asian common-law jurisdiction where English remains a second language to most of them and yet the primary medium of instruction of legal education, we suggest that legal educators have to contextualize this scheme against possible cultural and linguistic particularities. A number of inquiries remain to be addressed in the future, based on the above findings, if the SC programme is to be adopted as a long-term programme to teach and assess law students' communication and interviewing skills in Hong Kong, or perhaps also in other jurisdictions in Asia.

(1) Should we conduct one interview in Cantonese (an indigenous language) and one in English (a second and official language in legal education) for each student in each subject in order to mirror the two major client groups which lawyers in practice in Hong Kong would normally encounter in real life? If so, how are we going to accommodate the needs of English-speaking and Mandarin-speaking students who do not or cannot speak Cantonese?

(2) How do we eliminate the relative disadvantage in assessment suffered by local students versus their overseas classmates in an SC interview in English? If both SCs speaking in indigenous language and English are recruited to mirror the client mix of real legal practice, how do we ensure fairness in assessments of local and overseas students between these two groups of SCs?

(3) More fundamentally, do we see the assessment criteria on communicative competence devised overseas as reasonable criteria for client–lawyer communication in Hong Kong? Does the scoring rubric devised from and for a Scottish project represent what clients in Hong Kong, from a different culture with a different code of etiquette and perhaps lifestyle, expect from a lawyer and perceive in certain gestures? Communicative competence is an issue common to contemporary legal educators globally and it remains, we argue, a highly contextualized discourse that is inevitably shaped by cultural and jurisdictional particularities. Therefore, framing a jurisdictional specific scheme of teaching and assessing communicative competence, and fitting them with the language and cultural particularities of students, are of utmost importance to the reliable and sustainable operation of an SC programme, apart from securing necessary manpower and financial support, which are also indispensable for any innovation in experiential pedagogical tools.

Acknowledgements

The authors would like to thank the reviewers for their very constructive comments and ideas including, but not limited to, the following which bring about additional dimensions to future research on the SC programme: (a) contrast (or account for any difference) between a client interview (in WTEP) and a non-client/witness interview (in Civil Lit.) given that their respective motives and conflicts are presumably different; and (b) comparative studies with literature and/or datasets in another/broader field such as business communication.

Disclosure statement

No potential conflict of interest was reported by the authors.

Funding

This work was supported by the University of Hong Kong Teaching Development Grants 2012 and 2013.

Notes

[1] The majority of the full-time students in 2013/14 (251 students) are fresh graduates in the age range of 22–24 with a small number of mature students, while many part-time students have been working for a number of years. The oldest part-time student is 62 years old.

[2] Monash University School of Law, Melbourne, Australia; Brigham Young University Law School, Provo, Utah, US; New York University Law School, US; and Case Western Reserve University School of Law, Cleveland, Ohio, US (Barton *et al.*, 2006, p. 10).

[3] In a way, such comparison with existing published empirical analyses may not be entirely possible given the differences in objectives of these analyses. For example, Barton *et al.*'s paper focuses on comparing SCs' assessment with tutors' assessment to verify the validity and reliability of the former. IAALS's study uses SC interview results to assess the competence of DWS graduates over non-DWS lawyers. Fry *et al.*'s analyses, based on a much smaller sample size, show the possible correlation between students' pass rate in one clinical component (containing SC interviews and other tests) with students' background such as gender, language, etc. This paper will make a unique contribution to the field by empirically analysing students' performance in SC interviews and students' evaluation of the SC programme based on a relatively large sample size, and studying the possible correlation of the performance and evaluation with students' background.

[4] According to the Annual Report of the Standing Committee on Legal Education and Training (2014), for 2013/14, there were over 1,400 applicants.

[5] Source: Law List – www.hklawsoc.org.hk/pub_e/memberlawlist/mem_firm.asp (accessed 30 June 2014; the percentage was manually worked out by browsing the profile of all those firms that day). As at 30 June 2014, among 825 registered law firms in Hong Kong, about 72.4% of them are sole proprietorships or with no more than two partners.

[6] *Ibid.* As at 30 June 2014, around 70% of those firms did not have any legally qualified person other than the sole proprietors.

[7] In GGSL, three sessions of over 500 interviews were completed between January 2005 and January 2006. This observation is drawn from Barton *et al.*, supra note 3. The Australia National University has been running their own SC programme recently but it does not seem to have any report of data of this kind. To our best understanding, the scale there and the number of interviews completed are both smaller.

[8] Taking into account the suggestion, in the interviews held in February 2015, an SC gave immediate verbal feedback to a student in the one area which the SC thought the student had done the best or the worst in, with a short remark in addition to any written comment on the comment/assessment marking sheet.

[9] Most SCs are full-time housewives in their 40s–50s recruited through HKU faculty members' network. All of them have previous working experience and can speak fluent English. Although we did not conduct a structured survey of SCs' evaluation of the HKU's SC programme, informal conversations with SCs held during training sessions revealed their support of the programme and their satisfaction with their roles. Such support is also shown by the continuation in service of a large proportion of SCs in many subsequent rounds of SC exercises held from 2013 to 2015.

[10] Independent-samples *t*-test is a tool to test if there is a significant difference between the means of two separate groups of samples (George & Mallery, 2008). The *t*-value ($p < 0.05$) indicates an acceptable confidence interval (95%) for the mean difference (Field, 2009).

[11] In OSCE (2011), 81% of 21 men passed and 97% of 29 women passed. It is worth noting certain differences between OSCE of QLTS conducted in Kaplan Law School, UK and SC interviews conducted at HKU that make the above comparison less than perfect. Firstly, QLTS is a test for lawyers

already qualified in jurisdictions other than England and Wales who seek to practise in England and Wales, while SC assessment at HKU is for law students who are yet to enter into legal traineeship. Secondly, OSCE's results contain non-interview elements such as an oral presentation and preparation of an attendance note, while SC interviews in HKU only assess students' interviewing skills. Thirdly, the sample size of candidates sitting for that OSCE is relatively small (a total of 50 candidates).

[12] See Evans (2013), for such observations based on a survey on the use of English in Hong Kong involving 2,000 respondents.

[13] Again, as mentioned in note 11 above, certain differences between OSCE and SC interviews conducted at HKU make the above comparison less than perfect. To reiterate, firstly QLTS is a test for qualified lawyers. Secondly, OSCE's results contain non-interview components. Thirdly, HKU's SCs speak English either as their first or second language, while English presumably is the first language of all SCs used in OSCE. Finally, the sample size of candidates sitting for the OSCE work is relatively small.

[14] Although the hypothesis is confirmed by statistically significant improvement in marks in the second interview conducted in elective courses, the authors acknowledge that such confirmation could be further reinforced if a control group of students (who did not participate in the first SC interview) were compared with those who had carried out an interview before. However, under the practical circumstances of our curriculum, the formation of such a group was not possible because the first interview was mandatory for all students of Civil Lit., which is a compulsory course held during the first semester. Elective courses such as WTEP/ELP were only conducted in the second semester. The authors however do think that the results mentioned in Table 10 of this article are of significant empirical value, despite the absence of control.

[15] Rules of research ethics issued by HKU were followed when we implemented the student evaluation and prior approval on research ethics was obtained from the relevant authority of HKU (under Reference No. EA031010).

[16] See footnote 8 above for action taken, taking into account the suggestion expressed.

References

Barton, K., Cunningham, C., Jones, G. & Maharg, P. (2006) Valuing what clients think: standardized clients and the assessment of communicative competence, *Clinical Law Review*, 13(1), pp. 1–65.

Chow, W. & Ng, M. (2014) Standardized clients in Asia – University of Hong Kong's experience, in: F. Westwood & K. Barton (Eds) *Calling of Law: The Pivotal Role of Vocational Legal Education* (Surrey, UK, Ashgate Publishing Ltd), pp. 165–179.

Chow, W. & Tiba, F. (2013) Too many 'what's, too few 'how's, *European Journal of Law and Technology*, 4(1). Available at: http://ejlt.org//article/view/183/281.

Cronbach, L. & Shavelson, R. (2004) My current thoughts on coefficient alpha and successor procedures, *Educational and Psychological Measurement*, 64(3), pp. 391–418. doi:10.1177/0013164404266386

Cunningham, C. (1999) Evaluating effective lawyer-client communication: as international project moving from research to reform, *Fordham Law Review*, 67(5), pp. 1959–1986.

Cunningham, C. (2011) Should American law schools continue to graduate lawyers whom clients consider worthless? *Maryland Law Review*, 70, pp. 499–512.

Evans, D. (1989) Taken at the flood: Hong Kong's first law school, in: R. Wacks (Ed) *The Future of Legal Education and the Legal Profession in Hong Kong* (Hong Kong, Faculty of Law, University of Hong Kong), pp. 6–31.

Evans, S. (2013) Perspectives on the use of English as a business lingua franca in Hong Kong, *International Journal of Business Communication*, 50(3), pp. 227–252. doi:10.1177/0021943613487073

Field, A. (2009) *Discovering Statistics Using SPSS* (London, Sage Publications).

Fry, E., Crewe, J., & Wakeford, R. (2012) The qualified lawyers transfer scheme: innovative assessment methodology and practice in a high stakes professional exam, *The Law Teacher*, 46(2), pp. 132–145. doi:10.1080/03069400.2012.681174

Fry, E., Crewe, J., & Wakeford, R. (2013) Using multiple choice questions to examine the content of the qualifying law degree accurately and reliably: the experience of the Qualified Lawyers Transfer Scheme, *The Law Teacher*, 47(2), pp. 234–242. doi: 10.1080/03069400.2013.790156

Garvey, J.B., & Zinkin, A.F. (2009) Making law students client-ready: a new model in legal education, *Duke Forum for Law & Social Change*, 1, pp. 101–129.

Garvey, J.B. (2010) New Hampshire's performance-based variant of the Bar Examination: the Daniel Webster Scholar Honors Program moves beyond the pilot phase, *The Bar Examiner*, pp. 13–23.

Garvey, J.B. (2013) Making law students client-ready: the Daniel Webster Scholar Honors Program: a performance-based variant of the Bar Exam, *NYSBA Journal*, pp. 44–50.

George, D. & Mallery, P. (2008) *SPSS for Windows Step by Step: A Simple Guide and Reference, 15.0 Update* (Boston, Mass., Pearson A & B).

Grosberg, L. (2001) Medical education again provides a model for law schools: the standardized patient become standardized client, *Journal of Legal Education*, 51, pp. 212–234.

Grosberg, L. (2004) Standardized clients: a possible improvement for the bar exam, *Georgia State University Law Review*, 20(4), pp. 841–875.

Grosberg, L. (2006) How should we assess interviewing and counseling skills? *International Journal of Clinical Legal Education*, 9, pp. 57–72.

Institute for the Advancement of the American Legal System (IAALS). (2015) *Ahead of the Curve - Turning Law Students into Lawyers. A Study of the Daniel Webster Scholar Honors Program at the University of New Hampshire School of Law.* (Denver, IAALS).

Jen, J. (2009) *Curriculum Review Report 6 2008–2009* (Hong Kong, Department of Professional Legal Education, University of Hong Kong).

Maharg, P. (2011) Standardized clients @ Northumbria University Law School. Available at: http://paulmaharg.com/2011/09/16/standardized-clients-northumbria-university-law-school/, accessed March 2015.

Mula, A., Rowe, M., & Steed, A. (2012) *Final Report of 2011 Teaching Enhancement Grant – Standardised Client Initiative*. Available at: http://edcasestudies.chelt.anu.edu.au/sites/edcasestudies.chelt.anu.edu.au/files/project_reports/TEG_Report_final_SCIintitiative_Law.pdf, accessed March 2015.

Standardized client in Ireland. (2011) *Standardized Client Initiative Blog*, 7 September. Available at: http://zeugma.typepad.com/sci/2011/09/standardized-clients-in-ireland.html, accessed March 2015.

Standing Committee on Legal Education and Training. (2014). *Annual Report 2013*. Available at: http://www.sclet.gov.hk/eng/pdf/2013e.pdf.

Wallace, P. (1997) Following the threads of an innovation: the history of standardized in medical patients in medical education, *Caduceus*, 13(2), pp. 5–28.

Wallace, P. (2007) *Coaching Standardized Patients: For Use in the Assessment of Clinical Competence* (New York, Springer).

Willoughby, P. (1999) The postgraduate certificate in laws: some reminiscences, in: P. Wesley-Smith (Ed.) *Thirty Years: HKU Law School 1969–1999* (Hong Kong, Faculty of Law Publication, University of Hong Kong), pp. 42–43.

The National Lawyers College of the People's Republic of China

RODERICK O'BRIEN
School of Management, University of South Australia, Adelaide, Australia

ABSTRACT *The National Lawyers College of the People's Republic of China was established in Baoding City in 2012. This note examines the professional and governmental context for the college, the courses that have been presented, and the potential for the college as part of post-qualification education for China's lawyers.*

The newly established Lawyers College

In just a few decades, the number of lawyers in China has grown rapidly. There were Soviet-style lawyers in the early years of the People's Republic of China, but from the beginning of the anti-Rightist campaign in 1957 to the end of the Great Proletarian Cultural Revolution and its aftermath in 1979, the number of lawyers dwindled to a handful. From this very small renewal in 1979, the situation has changed dramatically. At the end of 2012 the All China Lawyers Association reported 232,384 lawyers, organised into 19,361 law firms. Continuing education for these lawyers is not forgotten, and there are a wide variety of programmes for this purpose. Under its constitution, the All China Lawyers Association itself has a responsibility for continuing education. But this task is also undertaken by universities, by some law firms and some other organs. A significant newcomer is the National Lawyers College.

For some years, China has had professional training colleges for judges, established by the Supreme Court, and for procurators, established by the Supreme Procuratorate. And there have been suggestions for a college for lawyers on an equal footing (Xue & Liu, 2013). Yu Ning, then President of the All China Lawyers Association, had made such a suggestion in 2008, citing the inability of law graduates to readily undertake legal practice. Then, in November 2012, the Ministry of Justice set up a National College for Lawyers (Ministry of Justice, 2012). The legal professions are usually considered as comprising judges, procurators, lawyers and notaries, and the Ministry of Justice is the responsible ministry for the regulation of lawyers and notaries. The new college was duly launched by the Minister of Justice Wu Aiying and Deputy Minister of Justice Zhao Decheng, along with a variety of officials from the Central Politics and Law Committee, other Ministry of Justice offices at national, provincial and local level, as well as cadres and lawyers (Wang, 2012). Also attending was the dean of the new institute, Wang Hengqin. In her address, Minister Wu referred to the establishment of the National Law School as a major event in the history of lawyers in China, marking a new stage in the development of China's legal education and training.

Minister Wu set the orientation for the new college firmly in the implementation of the policies of the Chinese Communist Party (Wu, 2013). She said that only from that orientation can the college fulfil its role in the training of lawyers, and build up the socialist legal system with Chinese characteristics. Minister Wu referred to a wide variety of training, including ideological training, ethical training and training lawyers for leading roles. One of the tasks for the college is to promote exchanges and co-operation with foreign lawyers: as some foreign training institutes have centuries of experience, this may be useful for the development of China's lawyers.

Some surprises

But whereas the colleges for judges and procurators are well-presented separate establishments in the suburbs of Beijing, the Ministry of Justice chose to locate its college in the relatively small city of Baoding in Hebei province, about 150 kilometres outside of Beijing. Baoding has a population of around one million in its urban areas, and is not even the provincial capital of Hebei province. That honour belongs to Shijiazhuang a further 150 kilometres away. Moreover, the Lawyers College is located at an existing training college for judicial police (prison guards), operated by the Ministry of Justice. The head of the new college is not a lawyer: the existing head of the training college, Wang Hengqin, has been given the added role of Dean of the Lawyers College. The uniformed brass band of the training college provided the music for the opening ceremony of the Lawyers College. Baoding at least has a history of training legal advisors in the nineteenth century, but it is unlikely that this influenced the choice of location for the new college (Chen, 2012).

Blogging lawyers were quick to comment on this surprising development, and gently mocked the new location and the background of the new dean as an official in charge of training judicial police (Tan, 2012; Fan, 2012). Certainly the establishment of the National Lawyers College in this manner sends a clear message that lawyers are not regarded by the Ministry of Justice in the same way as judges and procurators are regarded, with their own colleges in Beijing headed by their own professionals. Perhaps this is due to the fact that judges and procurators are still state functionaries, whereas most lawyers now work in law firms, 'unhooked' from the state. Lawyers may like to describe themselves as free professionals, on the European model, while the Ministry of Justice usually refers to them as "law workers for socialism with Chinese characteristics".

Co-location is not unusual in China. The situation is described as 'adding a name-plate'. There is another recent 'two-plate' institution for comparison: on 26

July 2013, the Beijing Lawyers College was opened on the same site as the Ministry of Justice Beijing Bureau Central Party School (Beijing City Justice Bureau, 2013). This urban institute has run its opening programme on the legal developments by the Chinese Communist Party (Zhicheng Public Interest Lawyers, 2013). Nevertheless, Liu Xiqiu, the managing partner of one Jiangxi law firm, commented that the National Lawyers College is neither fish nor fowl – "lawyers are lawyers, judicial police are judicial police, what is the relationship?" (Mu, 2014).

College programmes

Gradually the new college recruited staff, both internal and adjunct staff from law firms, and began its work. At the time of writing, the college has completed two courses, and is undertaking a third. Each course has been offered with 100 places, and these places are distributed across the country. For example, the Shanghai Lawyers Association offered up to three places for participants in the third course. These participants were expected to provide their own transportation to Baoding, but the instruction and accommodation were free. There are no public reports of other activities by the National Lawyers College.

On 27 May 2013, the college gave its first course with the themes of law firm management and lawyers' professional development (Ministry of Justice Net, 2013). Some 100 participants from different parts of China took part in the course. The head of the Ministry of Justice's political bureau Zhang Yanzheng gave the keynote address, in which he called lawyers "law workers for socialism with Chinese characteristics". The choice of law firm management as a theme responds to a great need among Chinese lawyers. While a few law firms are very well managed, and can be competitive with foreign lawyers, many of China's firms suffer from poor management. In 2009, the President of the Beijing Lawyers Association, Zhang Xuebing, said that he was concerned about "lack of professional ethics, overcharging clients, low efficiency, and not giving invoices" (Zhang, 2009). A significant number of disciplinary cases relate to infringement of practice management rules. While disciplinary cases necessarily show the negative side of the profession, some are instructive. In 2013 the Shenzhen Lawyers Association issued a disciplinary criticism for a law firm which was clearly not functioning properly. Some persons who had not qualified as lawyers were acting as partners, and participated in the partners' meetings and management. The law firm lacked proper documentation of its organisation, its financial system did not comply with the relevant rules, and management was disorganised. The partners insulted and even assaulted one another (Shenzhen Lawyers Association, 2013). The goal of the Ministry of Justice is to encourage law firms which are efficient, and which can withstand foreign competition. At present China protects its legal profession from competition by largely excluding foreign firms, but there is pressure from other countries to open up its service sectors, including law.

Lawyers came even from remote Xinjiang for the November 2013 five-day course relating to intellectual property (Jing, 2013). Again the topic was very relevant to developing the skills of China's lawyers. Internationally, China has long been known for paying little attention to the intellectual property of others. But this is now having internal consequences as some local industries are capable of significant industrial and commercial developments – but cannot protect these at home. In addition, the lack of protection for intellectual property is discouraging high-tech investment in China. During a 2005 interview with the German newspaper *Der Speigel*, Singapore's former Prime Minister Lew Kuan Yew identified a significant gap in China's potential. He said that the opportunities for countries such as Singapore could be found

> where the rule of law, intellectual property and security of production systems are required, because for them to establish that, it will take 20 to 30 years. We are concentrating on bio medicine, pharmaceuticals and all products requiring protection of intellectual property rights. No pharmaceutical company is going to go have its precious patents disclosed. So that is why they are here in Singapore and not in China. (Hoyng & Lorenz, 2005)

Nearly a decade after these remarks, China is still struggling to establish the rule of law, intellectual property and security of production systems. Forming a competent and well-trained legal profession is part of China's response.

The third course is planned to commence on 30 June 2014, concluding on 5 July. This course targets a relatively new and growing occupational group within China's lawyers, those who are in-house lawyers for governments. The teaching group includes the current President of the All China Lawyers Association, Wang Junfeng. Wang is well-known internationally as the founder, in 1993, of top-tier firm King and Wood. With China's rapidly growing trade and investment abroad, by both state-owned enterprises and private entrepreneurs, Wang has encouraged China's lawyers to globalise. King and Wood was one of the early firms to establish offices abroad. In recent years, the firm has entered a *verein* arrangement with Australian law firm Mallesons to become King Wood Mallesons.

There are no reports of other work than the three training courses.

The National Lawyers College and other continuing education providers

The National Lawyers College is entering a market where universities have already established lawyers' colleges in Beijing and other major cities. In addition, the All China Lawyers Association has the task of providing legal education for lawyers, and has considerable experience in this field. The All China Lawyers Association is organised in a hierarchy from a central organisation, to provincial, and to other levels such as cities, below the provincial level. Each level shares the responsibility for training. But there have been consistent criticisms of the quality of post-qualification training offered by the associations. These criticisms have been based on the lack of training plans, instructors and materials. The quality of training varies from location to location: well-funded associations such as in Shanghai seem to be able to provide better quality training (Ji, 2009).

There is debate as to the appropriate organ to be offering post-qualification training: some commentators have suggested that the All China Lawyers Association is the appropriate body. Nevertheless, there seems to be some level of co-operation. Thus the third course was advertised through local lawyers' associations, and the Beijing Lawyers Association has co-operated with the Beijing Lawyers College in running courses. Where both government and the lawyers' associations (relying on membership dues) are able to fund courses, there may be a better response than to a course based on fee-payment by participants (Mu, 2014).

In April 2014, the Lawyers College at the prestigious Renmin University convened a forum attended by 12 lawyers' colleges, including the National Lawyers College, and 12 representatives of the All China Lawyers Association from provincial levels (Lawyers College, 2014). Participants agreed that the growing trend of establishing ongoing education for lawyers in lawyers' colleges and universities is an inevitable trend, and is needed for the healthy development of lawyers. Participants called for the education of lawyers to be given national status, coming under the national education system as soon as possible. One of the results of the forum was to establish an association of lawyers' colleges and educators, and branches are being formed at the provincial level. The group has also established its own website (China Lawyer Inns, 2014). The name of the site is drawn from the Inns of Court. The endorsement of university-based colleges and colleges established by the Ministry of Justice at different levels would suggest that the All China Lawyers Association is not to have a monopoly on this work.

Conclusion

Because the field of post-qualification education already has some significant suppliers, the newly established National Lawyers College may not be a major event in the history of law in China, ushering in a new stage, despite the claims of the Minister for Justice. However, it certainly has potential. First, the themes chosen for the first three programmes are very relevant to the current situation of China's lawyers. Second, as a national college, the participants have been drawn from across China, and this could have a beneficial effect in raising the standards of lawyering in the central and western provinces, where legal resources are scarcer and less developed than in the more prosperous eastern provinces.

The National Lawyers College will have to establish its reputation: it may be handicapped by its location and administrative arrangements as a 'dual name-plate' with the judicial police training college. These can be overcome if the college can provide educators with high levels of both practical experience and the teaching skills to share that experience.

The rapid growth of lawyers' colleges and other forms of post-qualification education for lawyers is likely to be sustained. The formation of an association with the National Lawyers College as a participant may lead to better co-ordination in training.

Finally, the establishment of the National Lawyers College is grounded firmly in the maintenance of the policies of the Chinese Communist Party. These policies are driven by the Party and the state, rather than through the profession itself. The Party has set a particular direction, which controls the potential for development of the profession of lawyer, with a strong emphasis on technical competence as "law workers for socialism with Chinese characteristics".

Disclosure statement

No potential conflict of interest was reported by the author.

References

Beijing City Justice Bureau. (2013) City Bureau held the unveiling ceremony for the Beijing Institute of Lawyers and Central Beijing City Bureau of Justice Party School and part of the key lawyers training lecture, *Beijing City Justice Bureau*. Available at: www.bjsf.gov.cn/publish/portal0/tab68/info14357.htm, accessed 7 July 2014.

Chen, L. (2012) Legal specialists and judicial administration in late Imperial China, 1651–1911, *Late Imperial China*, 33(1), pp. 1–54.

China Lawyer Inns. (2014) China Lawyer Inns Net, *Lawyer Inns*. Available at: www.lawyerinns.com, accessed 7 July 2014.

Fan, K. (2012) Concerning the report "National Lawyers College", *Law Blog*. Available at: www.wxlaw.fyfz.cn/b/722631, accessed 7 July 2014.

Hoyng, H. & Lorenz, A. (2005) Spiegel interview with Singapore's Lee Kuan Yew: It's stupid to be afraid, *Der Spiegel*. 8 August. Available at: http://www.spiegel.de/international/spiegel/spiegel-interview-with-singapore-s-lee-kuan-yew-it-s-stupid-to-be-afraid-a-369128.html, accessed 7 July 2014.

Ji, Y. (2009) Present state and development prospect for legal education, in: Li (Ed) *Report on China's Legal Development No 7* (Beijing, Social Sciences Academic Publishing), p. 331.

Jing, T. (2013) Lawyers belonging to Xinjiang Lawyers Association attend intellectual property occupational training course, *Xinjiang Peace*. Available at: www.xjpeace.cn/lsls/201312/t20131204_124724.htm, accessed 7 July 2014.

Lawyer College, Renmin University of China. (2014) First Chinese lawyer education forum held, *Renmin University of China*. Available at: http://lawyer.ruc.edu.cn/html/xydt/8114.html, accessed 7 July 2014.

Ministry of Justice. (2012) The National Lawyers College is established, *Ministry of Justice*. Available at: www.moj.gov.cn/index/content/2012–12/21/content_4074257.htm?node=7343, accessed 7 July 2014.

Ministry of Justice Net. (2013) The National Lawyers College's first class begins: Wu Aiying and others attend the opening, *Central Peoples Government*. Available at: www.gov.cn/gzdt/2013–05/28/content_2412892.htm, accessed 7 July 2014.

Mu, Z. (2014) "The Biosphere of the Lawyers Colleges", *Fangyuan Luzheng*. Available at: http://www.fylz.com.cn/fylz/201406/201406/t20140630_1422823.shtml, accessed 4 September 2014.

Shenzhen Lawyers Association. (2013) Shenzhen lawyers disciplinary case 10 of 2013 Guangdong Shangda Law Firm is given a penalty of public criticism, *Shenzhen Lawyers Association*. Available at: www.szlawyers.com/info/ab59b81c5324406fa46cea955de3c029, accessed 7 July 2014.

Tan, M. (2012) Concerning several large puzzles and doubts on the establishment of the National Lawyers College, *Law Blog*. Available at: www.tanmintao.fyfz.cn/b/721882, accessed 7 July 2014.

Wang, K. (2012) The National Lawyers College is formally established: Wu Aiying chaired the opening ceremony and gave a speech, *Central Peoples Government*. Available at: www.gov.cn/jrzg/2012–12/20/content_2294936.htm, accessed 7 July 2014.

Wu, A. (2013) Conscientiously fulfil the functions of the National Lawyers College: carry forward the ranks of lawyers and develop the cause of lawyers, *Justice of China*, 2013(3). Available at: http://mall.cnki.net/magazine/Article/DDSF201303004.htm, accessed 7 July 2014.

Xue, Y. & Liu, X. (2013) Concerning the significance and conception of the establishment of the National Lawyers College, *21ccom*. Available at: www.21ccom.net/articles/zgyj/fzyj/article_2013092292336.html, accessed 7 July 2014.

Zhang, Y. (2009) City lawyers accused of unruly practice, *China Daily*, 3 December, p. 25.

Zhicheng Public Interest Lawyers. (2013) Wang Dan and Zhang Juan attend the unveiling ceremony for the Beijing Institute of Lawyers and Central Beijing City Bureau of Justice Party School and part of the key lawyers training lecture, *Zhicheng Public Interest Lawyers*. Available at: www.zcpi.org/a/news/ZhichengNews/2013/07/805.html, accessed 7 July 2014.

Index

Note: **Boldface** page number refer to figures and tables, Page number followed by n denotes endnotes.

INDEX

For Product Safety Concerns and Information please contact our EU
representative GPSR@taylorandfrancis.com
Taylor & Francis Verlag GmbH, Kaufingerstraße 24, 80331 München, Germany

www.ingramcontent.com/pod-product-compliance
Ingram Content Group UK Ltd.
Pitfield, Milton Keynes, MK11 3LW, UK
UKHW050055200926
475702UK00019B/2841
9780367139186